AI-Driven Value Management

AI-Driven Value Management

How AI Can Help Bridge the Gap Across the Enterprise to Achieve Customer Success

Craig LeGrande
Venky Lakshminarayanan

WILEY

Published by John Wiley & Sons, Inc., Hoboken, New Jersey.
Published simultaneously in Canada and the United Kingdom.

ISBNs: 9781394288823 (Hardback), 9781394288847 (ePDF), 9781394288830 (ePub)

For general information on our other products and services, please contact our Customer Care Department within the United States at (800) 762-2974, outside the United States at (317) 572-3993. For product technical support, you can find answers to frequently asked questions or reach us via live chat at https://support.wiley.com.

If you believe you've found a mistake in this book, please bring it to our attention by emailing our reader support team at wileysupport@wiley.com with the subject line "Possible Book Errata Submission."

Wiley also publishes its books in a variety of electronic formats. Some content that appears in print may not be available in electronic formats. For more information about Wiley products, visit our web site at www.wiley.com.

Library of Congress Control Number: 2024947776

Cover image: © Larysa Tsyvinska/Getty Images
Author photos: Courtesy of the author
Cover design: Wiley

SKY10091147_111524

Contents at a Glance

Contents

Foreword

Technology is advancing faster than I have ever seen in my 20+ years in technology. And although AI may seem like a new thing, technology leaders like IBM have been using it for a while. Computer scientist John McCarthy coined the phrase "artificial intelligence" in the 1950s. After that, in the 1960s IBM's CEO Thomas Watson, Jr.'s work centered on automating tasks, one of the hallmarks of today's AI. The 1970s were defined by statistical models and probability; while not exactly AI, elements certainly feed into them. Then in 1996, during the ultimate battle of human versus machine, an IBM computer called Deep Blue beat World Champion Garry Kasparov in chess. When I joined IBM in 1999, work was being done on rules-based engines and analytics, a precursor to IBM Watson, an AI computer that beat two *Jeopardy* champions in 2011. And since then, consistent progress every month and every year has brought AI to the forefront—leading IBM to introduce watsonx in 2023.

One thing is for certain: AI may not replace managers, but the managers who use AI will replace the managers who do not. It is the sure path to productivity, which is the sure path to growth. As I meet with clients daily, I have found a pretty successful formula for AI adoption to drive value: Foundation Models + Data + Governance + Use Cases.

Having model choice is really important. Sure, large language models have caught everybody's attention because of their direct consumer application. But for business, different models will be better at some tasks than they are at other tasks. The best model will depend on the industry, domain, use case, and size of model, meaning most will use many smaller large language models versus one larger model. Models pretrained on domain-specific data produce better results for businesses than general-purpose models. And with the right governance, companies can be assured that its workflows are compliant with ever-changing government regulations and free of bias. With this AI-driven value management system in place, business outcomes are achievable in record time.

Getting to the right outcomes starts with alignment of the leadership team on strategic intent. Having a long career leading large, high-powered sales teams, my experience tells me that the gold standard is building an aligned sales organization that can articulate the business value of product portfolios, first and foremost. Scaling this capability across products, regions, industries, and sales organizations can be challenging. To do so, AI will be a game changer as companies deploy AI to transform their internal functions, including go-to-market. Early wins are being seen as companies rely on AI-powered automation to optimize spend, improve operations, and drive greater financial returns.

In *AI-Driven Value Management*, you have a pragmatic handbook for understanding the magnitude of AI's potential to transform the way companies market, sell, and drive client success. Both Craig and Venkat have had a front row seat for this change, and hence they can be your tour guides in what is to come.

The world's best days are yet to come if we allow technology to flourish responsibly.

—Rob Thomas

Rob Thomas is Senior Vice President Software and Chief Commercial Officer, IBM. He leads IBM's software business, including product management and design, product development, and business development. In addition, Rob has global responsibility for IBM revenue and profit, including worldwide sales, strategic partnerships, and ecosystem.

In his over 20 years at IBM, Rob has held roles in IBM Consulting, IBM Microelectronics, and IBM Software. In 2007, Rob joined IBM's software business, focused on data and analytics. He held a variety of roles, including product engineering and business development, leading IBM's transition from databases to delivering broader analytical capabilities, investing in open source, and eventually artificial intelligence. Rob has overseen numerous acquisitions by the firm, representing over $12 billion in transaction value.

Introduction

This book is the culmination of 50 years of the authors' combined professional experience working in diverse roles as buyers, sellers, and builders of information technology systems. Over that period, Craig LeGrande and Venky Lakshminarayanan have seen big wins, big mistakes, and big lessons learned in the world of value management.

As a management consultant at Accenture and as a business value consultant at Cisco Systems, Craig mastered the art and science of showing the real impact of technology to executives. Selling based on hype or vague assumptions, he quickly discovered, was the fastest way to lose their interest. Says Craig: "Clients kept nagging me with questions like, 'How will your solution actually drive that kind of impact?' and 'Can my company really achieve those results?'"

Often, Craig was surprised by the lack of solid evidence to back up the claims of technology companies and consultants. "Many vendors exaggerated the benefits to the point that CFOs and CIOs would laugh at the numbers," Craig says. "It became clear to me that the only way to sell effectively was to build trust, stick to conservative estimates of business impact, and share real-life success stories."

When he left Cisco, Craig's first client was Oracle, who at the time was going head-to-head with software giant SAP in the enterprise resource planning (ERP) space. The company's CEO, Larry Ellison, had encouraged his sales team to develop a library of key performance indicators (KPIs) to definitively prove the benefit of Oracle's products. Partnering with Oracle to develop that messaging and support their sales teams was the launching pad for Craig's next career move—founding Main-stay with the mission of helping companies quantify and communicate the true business value of technology.

Venky Lakshminarayanan followed a similar career path. A couple decades ago, he was fortunate enough to find himself at the intersection of business and technology in Silicon Valley, which had become the epi-center of massive technology-led business transformations. He cut his teeth at PwC, working on large, multiyear projects involving ERP, supply chain, and customer relationship management (CRM) software solutions.

Back then, enterprise technology was all about selling product features—purely functional capabilities that we often referred to as "speeds and feeds." "It seemed like good customer testimonials were the only way to demonstrate business value," Venky says. "As I shifted into sales roles, I often wondered what that single factor is that could help us consistently win deals."

While Venky and his colleagues won a lot of deals, they also lost some. After one promising sale escaped their grasp, a CIO told him, "Your solution was probably the best, but we couldn't articulate its business value to our CFO." That was Venky's lightbulb moment. "I realized then that business value is the real currency—the driving force—of the tech industry. That's what led me to join Mainstay," he recalls.

Although the practice of value management was by and large a novelty when he arrived at Mainstay in 2010, the boutique consulting company was already breaking new ground in value management, evolving it into a science with predictable business outcomes. "I had the chance to work with global technology providers and their customers to understand and articulate the ROI of their investments," he says.

Later, while at ServiceNow—a Fortune 500 company that's been named one of the world's most innovative companies—Venky worked with an incredible team to build a companywide value management program that boosted pipeline, revenue, renewals, and customer expan-sion. Now, as chief revenue officer and president at Cron AI, a pioneer in autonomous technology, he is once again pushing the boundaries of what's possible with a value-based selling approach. "Quantifying and communicating value is still at the heart of everything we do," he says. "I believe value management is essential for every customer-facing function."

What's Inside

This book unveils the transformative role artificial intelligence can play in helping enterprise B2B companies build a thriving value management practice. It tackles the challenge of how to scale business value activities across all customer-facing business functions—minus the exorbitant costs—and equips business leaders with AI-integrated strategies to secure a competitive edge and generate significant revenue growth.

We show how AI can help businesses bridge the gap between its sales, marketing, and customer success teams, empowering them to communicate value in an integrated fashion, driving consistency and uniformity throughout the customer life cycle. To help companies implement this new value management strategy, this book provides a playbook for what this future should look like, how to get there, and its impact on business-to-business companies.

AI-Driven Value Management is your guide to designing a unified marketing and sales program across all customer-facing business functions. Inside, you will find a clear and actionable blueprint for achieving scalable, impactful business outcomes through advanced AI-powered value management strategies.

We argue that companies that adopt an AI-driven value management (AI-VM) approach can finally achieve the holy grail in customer relationships—a single, unified value management framework that we call *One Value Motion*. These companies will be able to articulate their solutions' customer outcomes and show customer success throughout their life cycle clearly and with remarkable precision.

We believe the use of *AI-Driven Value Management* strategies and tools will deliver transformational revenue growth for B2B enterprises across industries. In fact, we have already shown how companies with strong value management programs, augmented by AI, can double sales leads, double win rates, and reduce customer churn by half—leading to an overall 8X overall revenue improvement.

When companies combine the power of AI with modern value management tools and technologies, current barriers to revenue and customer growth, such as cost, resource constraints, and operational friction, can be eliminated—making these results easier and faster to achieve. We are confident that the AI-VM strategies, use cases, and real-world stories in this book will provide leaders with the tools they need to successfully harness AI-driven value management in their industries.

Who Should Read This Book

Whether you're a business leader, seasoned professional, or a curious business and technology enthusiast, you are sure to benefit from this exploration into the future of value management and artificial intelligence.

This book will be a valuable resource for everybody from C-suite executives to sales, marketing, and customer success leaders to day-to-day practitioners of value management. It will serve as a useful handbook for any customer-facing executive who sells technology solutions to businesses. In fact, you'll find useful stories, lessons, and advice from many of these leaders in the pages ahead.

CHAPTER

1

Introduction to AI-Driven Value Management

The rise of value management as an established business practice has been decades in the making. Yet it remains an evolving and dynamic field, as our businesses continue to modernize and digitize in surprising new directions.

As a result, long standing dogmas for selling products and services to business customers are being shattered in the process.

In this chapter, we'll briefly explore how value management came to be as a successful enterprise selling strategy and then more recently as a driver of marketing campaigns, customer loyalty programs, and partner ecosystems. We'll look at how more companies today are demanding better returns from their business investments, and we'll examine the tectonic shift in customer relationships that is forcing sellers in nearly every industry to deliver tangible and recurring business value to the buyers of their products.

Finally, we'll introduce the game-changer: Artificial intelligence (AI) in all its forms and its potential for bringing the selling power of value management to more parts of the business, at lower cost, and at unprecedented speed and scale. We conclude with this book's bold thesis: That combining the power of AI with a state-of-the-art value management approach can empower businesses to realize 8X revenue outcomes.

A Brief History of Value Management

In the late 1940s, managers at the emerging industrial powerhouse General Electric (GE) were searching for ways to maximize business value by optimizing how the company deployed its scarce raw materials and human resources.[1] The methods developed by GE were refined into a formal methodology and the term *value management* was born. Since then, value management has steadily grown in popularity, becoming a highly useful sales technique for many companies seeking to sell complex, high-cost products and services to customers in a wide range of industries.

In recent decades, the practice has continued to attract followers among business-to-business (B2B) companies, especially in the high-technology arena. We've seen the emergence of this trend firsthand working for large systems implementers and high-tech companies since the late 1990s. Without realizing it, we found ourselves on the front lines of the tech wars, helping our clients take advantage of the latest value management methods. By then, information technology (IT) had risen to the status of strategic investment for more and more enterprises, and the chief information officer (CIO)—finally—had gained a seat at the executive table. With large sums at stake, corporate leaders began asking an obvious question: Exactly how much business value are we going to get from these massive technology investments?

To keep their customers happy and their sales surging, technology vendors were determined to answer that question. Many chose to hire teams of management consultants (sometimes referred to as *business value consultants* or *business value engineers*) to get a monetary handle on the business value of their products and thus gain access to executive buy-in. These teams specialized in translating technical specifications and product features into the language of business outcomes. The *customer value assessments* they produced—commonly called business cases—soon became an integral part of the sales cycle for the company's most valuable prospects. The consultants often worked closely with sales leadership and the executive team to help customers justify large-scale technology investments and support their customers' capital investment process.

By the 2010s, the practice of value management had become a widely accepted *sales overlay*, a team of specialists supporting the sales team. The success of these teams in closing the largest and most strategic deals started attracting new converts in product marketing and in

---

[1] "Strategic Value Management," PMI, Michel Thiry, PhD, PMP, PMI Fellow, (https://www.pmi.org/learning/library/strategic-value-management-business-benefits-8699).

customer success organizations. These business functions were interested in building value messaging "upstream," where it could inform the customers early in their decision-making process, as well as "downstream," where it could drive subscription renewals, broaden the customer life cycle, and boost revenue streams.

However, in recent years, many value management initiatives have hit a budget wall. Stubbornly high costs—especially the expense of using highly paid business value consultants—have been a barrier to growing value management programs or expanding into other functions. Fragmented organizational structures—and their associated politics— can also make it difficult to expand these initiatives to other functions, such as marketing, professional services, and customer success. What's more, although more companies have access to robust digital tools to streamline customer research and analyses, they are often deployed in piecemeal fashion and fall short of reaching the overall goals of these platforms. Taken together, these costs and inefficiencies can create structural impediments to scaling value management programs across the enterprise and enabling companies to capture the potential of end-to-end value management.

Then, seemingly overnight, the world changed. The arrival of generative artificial intelligence (GenAI) in the form of ChatGPT and a plethora of other AI technologies and apps sent shockwaves through the digital economy and sparked a full-fledged cultural phenomenon. There appears to be no limit to AI's potential to radically disrupt the way companies do business, from designing and manufacturing products exponentially faster to providing customer service that is uncannily human.

Companies seeking to build an enterprise value management program will be prime beneficiaries of the AI revolution, adding incredible speed, automation, and economies of scale to what are currently highly manual, error-prone, and costly processes. To introduce the opportunity of AI, let's look back at how far we've come with this technology.

The Evolution of AI

As early as the 1950s, rule-based or classical AI was developed for symbolic manipulation and logic to mimic human decision-making. The 1980s saw the advent of neural networks, which introduced the concept of learning from data by simulating the interconnectedness of neurons in the human brain. And since the early 2000s, with the availability of computing power at lower and lower costs, we've seen rapid strides in predictive AI or machine learning. This has enabled us to build algorithms that learn from data to make predictions or decisions without being explicitly programmed.

Though it has been around for more than a decade, GenAI burst into the limelight in 2023. GenAI can generate new content such as images, text, or music, often indistinguishable from human-created content. Another emerging area of interest is *agentic AI*, also called *autonomous AI*, which can act independently, making decisions and taking actions in complex environments without human intervention. The AI capability that can create scale for value management today is a combination of predictive AI and GenAI.

For now, GenAI is in its infancy. But we already can envision how and what this new technology can do to generate a new wave of opportunity for value management. As companies struggle to extend their value management programs to the whole enterprise, GenAI offers a practical solution that any B2B company, following a set of proven strategies and techniques, can master.

This book provides that blueprint. It begins with examples of currently successful value management programs and shows how GenAI solutions can take these programs further, empowering more parts of the business and unlocking significant new revenue opportunities. This book also draws a road map highlighting key phases of an ideal deployment that ensures successful business outcomes and minimizes common traps that we've seen delay or stall previous value management initiatives.

HOW GENERATIVE AI POWERS VALUE MANAGEMENT

Wikipedia defines GenAI as "artificial intelligence capable of generating text, images, videos, or other data using generative models, often in response to natural language prompts." GenAI's role in OpenAI's blockbuster ChatGPT is just one example of how this technology is redefining society. It is now finding its role in a myriad of business applications, including marketing, sales, and more recently, value management programs. For example, if integrated well into a company's existing sales workflow, GenAI capabilities can help a B2B seller to:

- Automate email responses and actions
- Summarize documents, text, and videos
- Document question and answer (Q&A)
- Analyze and aggregate data

- Visualize data (e.g., charts, infographics)
- Convert text to speech
- Inform/provide Q&A for images and charts
- Convert text to images
- Convert text to collaborative workflows
- Convert text to code actions
- Analyze sentiment
- Translate communications
- Review and summarize documents

These AI capabilities and thousands more can be customized to match the unique workflows of different industries and integrated into existing sales operations. Its potential for automating and accelerating critical tasks can help reduce costs and enable organizations to successfully scale value management programs throughout the enterprise.

WHAT IS VALUE MANAGEMENT?

Simply put, *value management* is the art and science of orchestrating the business functions within your enterprise to maximize business value for your customers. It encompasses a range of practices aimed at identifying, creating, and sustaining value throughout all aspects of the business. True value management requires all parts of the enterprise to come together around a common vision and purpose. Consequently, a unified value management program is the best way for B2B providers to grow their revenue and maximize customer loyalty.

Modern Corporate Governance—Raising the Bar on Capital Investments

Over the past few decades, corporate boards have tightened the reins on how their companies are operated and what investments they make. As a result, the practice of *corporate governance*, especially for large public institutions, has matured significantly. Boards of directors and top executives have implemented robust and highly structured investment committees and policies to ensure maximum return on invested capital.

In many ways, these modern investment-management structures have served to "pull" B2B companies toward adopting value management programs. These large enterprises, in turn, have encouraged their vendors to adopt value management programs to help them build return on investment (ROI) business cases and provide other analyses needed to meet their investment requirements.

The authors witnessed this firsthand, living and working at the intersection of technology and business for the last three decades. Over this time, we've seen the magnitude of technology investments skyrocket in every industry, becoming the single largest capital investment for most companies.

To better manage their budding portfolio of tech investments, company executives raised the bar on what projects could get funding. They started asking top managers to show the actual return on investment for new projects before greenlighting them. Many established a program management office (PMO) to identify, assess, and manage large IT investment opportunities as part of their overall capital investment planning process. As the Project Management Institute (PMI)® reports,[2] this "evolved PMO" was a "full-service PMO that supports and aligns strategic, tactical, and operational considerations." Investments codified and prioritized by this management body were then reviewed and approved by the board of directors.

The growing adoption of the new and improved PMO changed how many large companies procured new technologies and spurred the establishment of more rigorous investment standards. This had serious consequences for technology vendors: it meant that in order to close deals, they would have to provide their would-be customers with clear economic justification for their products and services.

Rethinking Customer Relationships

Selling to customers became even more challenging as more B2B companies began transitioning from product-based companies to software as a service (SaaS) companies. In simple terms, SaaS companies sell *subscriptions* to their software, with users paying a recurring fee; product companies require a one-time payment for indefinite use of their products.

---

[2] Giraudo, L. & Monaldi, E. (2015). PMO evolution: From the origin to the future. Paper presented at PMI® Global Congress 2015—EMEA, London, Project Management Institute (www.pmi.org/learning/library/pmo-evolution-9645).

Realizing the profound significance of this shift, we wrote *Competing for Customers* (Pearson FT Press, 2016). It was clear to us that as the subscription economy became mainstream, sellers would need to connect with their customers at a deeper level and forge more enduring relationships. In other words, they would be forced to become *customer-first companies*.

This meant SaaS companies would need to rethink how they engaged customers—at every level. Instead of being rigidly focused on closing deals, they would need to think more holistically by tracking and engaging customers throughout their life cycle—an extended relationship that spans initial awareness of a company's brand all the way to contract renewals.

It's been proven that taking a customer-first approach pays off. Companies that adopted this model delivered 35 percent better stock performance compared to the S&P 500 over an 8-year period, and nearly 80 percent better stock performance compared to late adopters of products.[3]

Since our book was published, the digital subscription economy has grown even faster than imagined. In fact, Swiss banking giant UBS predicts the subscription economy revenue will hit $1.5 trillion by 2025, and Statista reports that key market segments such as cloud computing are expected to double in size from 2020 to 2025, reaching $536 billion (see Figure 1.1).[4] As we detailed in *Competing for Customers*, customers in the subscription-based economy command greater leverage over their vendors, since switching costs are relatively low and sellers need to make good on their promises to retain their business.

The Road to Customer First

However, what we failed to appreciate at the time was just how difficult it would be for companies to transform themselves into a customer-first company. The book explored different ways to help companies bridge the gap—for example, by launching a new business function known as a *customer success organization*. This new corporate function would focus on ensuring that customers realized—in measurable ways—the business benefits promised by the seller. Since the book was published,

---

[3] *Competing for Customers* (Pearson, 2016), Figure 1.1, p. 12.
[4] "Market size of the digital subscription economy worldwide in 2020, with a forecast for 2025, by segment", Statistica, 2024 (https://www.statista.com/statistics/1295064/market-size-digital-subscription-economy-worldwide-by-segment).

thousands of companies have stood up similar organizations and successfully reduced customer churn as a consequence.

Market size of the digital subscription economy worldwide in 2020, with a forecast for 2025, by segment
(in billion U.S. dollars)

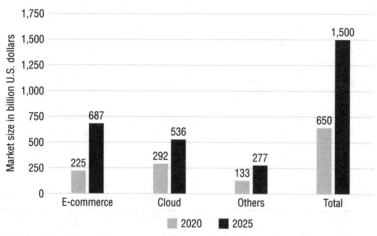

Figure 1.1: Subscription mania: Estimated growth of digital subscription economy worldwide

Customer success teams were off to a good start in helping realize value for their customers, but mostly their scope was too narrow, focusing mainly on reducing day-to-day technical and operational issues. Too often, these teams neglected to address the bigger task of *value realization*—that is, helping customers to track and quantify the achievement of their overarching business goals, such as greater sales, market share, and brand awareness.

Value management has never been more important in a market where customers devote an increasing share of their budgets to enterprise technologies, where buying cycles are longer and more complex, and where subscription-based business models are requiring vendors and customers to renew their original sales agreements every two or three years.

VM PRO TIP

To ensure customer success, and close more deals and renewals, technology sellers need to provide clear line of sight into how their technology solutions will deliver measurable business value for their customers.

The growing popularity of value management is not just a technology-industry phenomenon. Virtually all large enterprise investment decisions are being put through the same prioritization gauntlet. Other industries impacted include manufacturing, financial services, life sciences, automotive, utilities, government agencies, and many more. In order for B2B companies to outcompete in a subscription economy, they will need to create meaningful differentiation in the market. They can do this by adopting modern value management practices that achieve three basic outcomes:

- Provide clarity around the promised value before the purchase
- Grow pipelines and win deals
- Demonstrate realized value post-purchase to secure successful renewals and expand share of wallet

Resource Barriers

The road to becoming a value-centric customer-first company hasn't always been easy—or cheap. Indeed, many value management leaders have funded massive corporate programs to get there. Historically, implementing value management has been a resource-intensive exercise that takes years to mature.

At the core of the value management program has been the business value consultant. This is an expert who leads the effort to build *value models*—the financial and strategic template used to quantify and communicate the product's value for the customer—and create business cases to help provide economic justification for the investment. As you can imagine, these consultants spend a lot of time conducting research and analysis, building models, and doing collaborative reviews. Much of the work is manual, tedious, and difficult to automate.

Not surprisingly, value management consultants can be expensive. Typically, they are experienced professionals who have worked for top management consulting firms, have earned MBAs, and spent years in the industry cultivating relationships with executive-level buyers. For most companies, using value management consultants to support every sales opportunity would be inordinately expensive, especially for enterprise-level companies that field thousands of sales reps and an even larger set of partner sellers.

Thus, as companies seek to reap more benefits from value management by supporting more opportunities and customer accounts, they invariably run into a resource barrier. Fortunately, there is a way out of this dilemma by using new strategies, processes, and technologies, including AI, to scale value management efficiently and affordably.

Scaling Out Value Management

Since *Competing for Customers* was published, we've seen huge strides in the evolution of information technology. Key developments include:

- Advanced SaaS applications that have introduced best-of-breed workflows and tools for marketing, sales, and customer success
- Business processes supercharged with a wealth of analytics and insights from large datasets that help companies forecast, track, and measure how customers use products to capture benefits
- New value-automation platforms that provide fast, standardized ways to model, quantify, and communicate value to buyers

Together, these advances have opened the door to new opportunities for accelerating value management programs and more quickly delivering customer success. A number of forward-thinking enterprises—we'll look at several in the chapters ahead—have launched high-profile initiatives to leverage these advancements, allowing them to cost-effectively scale value-based programs, empower more business teams, win more sales opportunities, and retain more customers.

Recently developed *value management platforms*—soon to be empowered by GenAI—are helping these innovators standardize tasks and accelerate business case development. Enterprise sales teams using the platform's *value tools* can create integrated value-management workflows that help any sales team match the work of experienced value management consultants. What's more, the platform allows organizations to extend value management practices to groups adjacent to sales, such as marketing and customer success, and ultimately bring the advantages of value management to every part of the business.

Introducing the Value Management Life Cycle

The following chapters will detail the blueprint for creating an AI-powered value management program. The core goal for value management is to answer the following four simple questions for the customer:

- What value *can* I get?—Value opportunity
- What value *will* I get?—Value target

- What value *did* I get?—Value realized
- What *additional value* can I get?—Value expansion

This is the structure of how we'll take you on the journey. First, we will lay out how value management touches the customer in each of these life cycle stages and highlight the current challenges companies face as they try to build these capabilities. We'll then highlight how a company can leverage best practices, automation tools, and AI solutions to overcome these challenges and realize revolutionary company outcomes (e.g., revenue lift, margin expansion, reduced customer churn). The life cycle of the value management journey is illustrated in Figure 1.2.

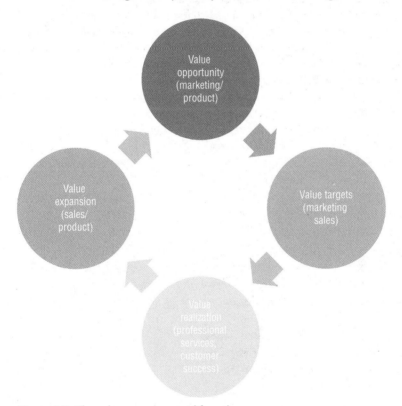

Figure 1.2: The value management life cycle

Your Guide to Achieving 8X Company Revenue Outcomes

The book is a guide for anyone interested in delivering a best-in-class value management program, including CEOs, sales, product, marketing, and customer success leaders, as well as experienced value management practitioners. No matter where you are in your value management journey, this book gives you the blueprint to build a company-wide unified value management program by integrating GenAI to drive exponential increases to your bottom line—a result we call *2-to-the-power-of-3, or 8X,* business revenue outcomes.

"2-TO-THE-POWER-OF-3" COMPANY REVENUE OUTCOMES

Companies implementing our AI-driven value management approach are seeing a quantum leap in revenue growth as well as measurable improvements across a gamut of sales, marketing, and customer success metrics. Based on our research, we conservatively estimate that B2B businesses that adopt our blueprint can expect to achieve what we call *2-to-the-power-of-3 revenue growth outcomes*: 2X pipeline, 2X revenue, and 2X LTV (customer lifetime value) expansion with lower churn and higher upsell and cross-sell rates.

The following chapters will dig deeper into this value formula and explore what it can mean for B2B companies across industries.

## CHAPTER 2

The Current State of Value Management

Chapter 1, "Introduction to AI-Driven Value Management," proposed the concept of value management and how it can help B2B businesses boost sales and retain more customers in today's subscription economy. In this chapter, we will discuss the current state of value management programs, deconstructing key value management activities and the complexities and challenges facing them. By establishing a baseline of how value management is practiced today, we will be able to establish a contrast to the future of value management powered by AI.

Understanding the Fundamentals of Business Value

At its highest level, business value can be described as a set of beneficial customer outcomes that drive competitive advantage, improve operational and financial performance, and result in positive impacts on employees, customers, shareholders, or the community.

Value management is relatively new to a lot of B2B companies and some are just experimenting with the practice. At many companies, you'll find pockets of teams using value management approaches intermixed with teams that follow traditional product feature-and-function go-to-market strategies. This can be confusing to sales teams, partners, and customers alike. Let's explore the difference between these two approaches.

Product Features vs. Value Messaging

The traditional sales pitch is primarily focused on promoting your product's best features—and it can sometimes be effective when your product or solution is straightforward and addresses a simple business problem, like a hammer that solves the problem of driving in a nail. However, this is rarely the case at large B2B enterprises that sell sophisticated solutions designed for complex, capital-intensive operating environments. These solutions often require the help of technical experts to integrate multiple products, design customized system configurations, and oversee installations that can take from months to years to complete. Given these challenges, there is no obvious or clear connection between the product's features and the business outcomes they are meant to deliver.

For these reasons, we believe that feature-based narratives are a poor strategy for selling or marketing enterprise-level B2B solutions. One of the most common mistakes these companies make is to get "too close" to their own products and simply assume that product descriptions alone are sufficient to communicate business value to their prospects. Unfortunately, these one-dimensional approaches can come across as marketing fluff and turn off business decision-makers and finance executives.

What's worse, feature-based selling often relies on technical jargon that can confound decision-makers looking for evidence of positive business impact. Gaining the attention of these critical *buyer personas* can be difficult when they can't grasp how these features relate to their specific business needs. Without a clear picture of how and what the product features do to address these challenges, the buyer will often mothball a deal until a clear benefits picture is established.

Table 2.1 shows the difference between features-based and value-based sales and marketing messages.

Table 2.1:   Features vs. Value: Two Kinds of Messaging

FEATURE-BASED PROPOSITIONS	VALUE-BASED PROPOSITIONS
Highlights your product's specific features, specifications, and technical aspects	Emphasizes the customer benefits and business outcomes that your product or service will provide
Involves detailed explanations of what your product does and its various functionalities	Focuses on solving your customer's problems and how the product can address an existing business challenge
May not directly address your customer's problems or quantify the business outcomes from deploying the product	Conversations revolve around your customer's needs and how the product adds value

How Value Beats Features: An Industry Success Story

Here's how a value-focused sales strategy helped a global networking company get through to its customers. The company had been on a buying spree, snapping up 12 companies to bolster its cybersecurity business. But selling this new collection of products was slow going, mainly because the jumble of solutions lacked a unifying business-value narrative, leaving the customers scratching their head over how everything fit together. Sales suffered as a result.

To reverse the slumping sales trend, the company's sales director kicked into gear, working with his product managers to develop a unified value narrative for the portfolio. The team's value-based approach aligned the products to their customers' three largest cybersecurity challenges—user security, cloud security, and breach protection—and knitted the portfolio together with business-outcome messages that customers could relate to. Customer interactions quickly turned from complex, often disjointed conversations about technical features and functions to productive discussions about how the customer can transform its business.

This is just one example of how value beats features in most B2B selling situations. But convincing the customer to invest in an expensive, resource-intensive solution takes more than just good communications. Most large enterprise buyers today are reluctant to pull the trigger without conducting a formal review to ensure any large financial outlay aligns with the company's strategic goals, financial targets, and risk management guidelines. This is where B2B sellers need to up their game—and dig deeper into the value management playbook—if they plan on closing more deals.

VALUE MANAGEMENT LEXICON

B2B businesses use a myriad of terms to describe the practice of value management. For sales, value engineers, customer success managers, and even company executives, having a well-grounded knowledge of these terms is critical to the success of value management programs.

- Business objectives, business imperatives (e.g., competitive advantage, strategic goals, long-range plans)
- Business case, business value assessment, customer value assessment, ROI case, value hypothesis, value forecast, value perspective
- ROI analysis, value analysis, value intelligence
- Value tree, value model, value framework, ROI model
- Strategic road map, value road map
- Value management consultant, value engineer, value strategist, value adviser, business value analyst

Refer to a full list of value management concepts in the Glossary.

The Modern Corporate Buying Process

Imagine you're the CFO of a Fortune 500 company and your company is facing a tough choice between three investment options: either you buy a multimillion-dollar computer and networking system, make a strategic business acquisition, or stand up a new factory. These are all big investments, and they carry big risks. So how do you make an informed decision that best supports your business?

You can start by putting together an investment committee to evaluate key factors, such as your strategic objectives, expected business results, resource requirements, and risks related to each investment. The committee will likely include people from corporate strategy, financial planning and audit, and the all-important program management office (PMO). They are there to help you develop a business rationale for the investment and monitor and manage the investment over its lifetime.

If it's a particularly large and strategic capital investment, most likely your board of directors will want to get involved.

Even before these investment options make it to the capital investment committee, you seek input from several middle-management decision-makers. In the case of a new assembly line robotic system, for example, a manufacturer is likely to rely on opinions from the following managers and executives:

- **Manufacturing line engineer:** Does the product drive additional throughput for our existing operations?

- **Plant manager:** How will the new robotic solution meet future demand and how does it improve the economics of my plant over the next 3–5 years?

- **Corporate financial analyst:** What are the capital expenditures (CapEx) and operating expenses (OpEx) impacts to this plant and its ability to scale out to other plants over the next 5–10 years?

- **Budget and forecasting manager:** How does this investment opportunity rank against other investments in the plant or across the business?

- **Chief operating officer (COO):** Do you trust the economics and operational forecasts by our team, and how does this investment align with our strategic priorities?

VALUE MANAGEMENT: GIVING YOU THE CONFIDENCE TO MOVE FORWARD

Investing in a large IT project can give a lot of buyers cold feet. But smart value management practices can provide the confidence they need to pull the trigger. "Many CIOs are faced with common challenges such as limited budgets, internal resources, and delivering high performing digital services to our constituents," says Bob Lim, CIO at San Jose State University. "Well-executed and flexible value management practices by my vendors and partners accelerate my ability to convince my leadership of the efficacy of an IT investment and gives me the confidence to move forward. Tight coordination and alignment between my IT team, the tech vendor, and system integrator (SI) is critical to gaining budget support and delivering on the business outcomes promised from the solution."

WHAT TO ASK BEFORE YOU INVEST

Today, most enterprise B2B companies follow a formal investment vetting process that poses a set of questions that decision-makers must answer for each and every opportunity presented to the business. These include:

- **Problem identification:** "We need to do something."

- **Solution exploration:** "What's out there to solve our problem?"

- **Requirements building:** "What exactly do we need the purchase to do?"

- **Supplier selection:** "Does this do what we want it to do?"

- **Validation:** "We think we know the right answer, but we need to be sure."

- **Consensus creation:** "We need to get everyone on board."

The Rise of PMOs

Over the last two decades, most large B2B companies have created a program management office (PMO) to address their long-term strategic planning needs. The PMO is charged with establishing the capital investment management process, designing and leading cross-functional decision-making committees, and reporting on investment portfolio performance.

The modern PMO sets a high bar for B2B vendors, extending the sales cycle by requiring detailed responses to questions around expected product performance and business value. According to HubSpot,[1] a typical SaaS sales cycle is around 84 days: "For an ACV (annual contract value) of less than $5,000, the cycle will last around 40 days. If the ACV is upwards of $100,000, the cycle will last 170 days—around five and a half months." Our experiences with enterprise buyers confirm this estimate, highlighting how much time and resources sellers need to commit to their customers' buying processes. Here are some of the top issues a PMO will want to explore with the vendor when evaluating a big purchase:

> **Strategic Alignment**   First and foremost, the investment must be a business priority for the buyer. For example, if an auto manufacturer is looking to invest in electric vehicles, bringing a new

---

[1] https://blog.hubspot.com/sales/saas-sales-ultimate-guide#:~:text=How%20long%20is%20a%20SaaS,will%20last%20around%2040%20days.

carburetor to the vendor may not make the cut. A PMO will often rank investments based on whether they will move the needle in line with where the business is headed strategically.

Operational Improvements   Many buyers are focused on optimizing one or more parts of their operations. So the PMO will often ask the vendor for a detailed assessment of the customer's current business processes, look for an explanation of how its product or service will improve that operation, and get a sense for the magnitude of that improvement. Ideally, the vendor could address these questions by pulling together existing customer success benchmarks, proposing proof-of-concept or pilot programs, and offering credible assurances that the company will be able to monitor the success of the solution throughout its lifetime.

Labor Impacts   Labor costs can make up as much as 50–70 percent of a business's total annual expenses. If the proposed investment can help to scale an existing labor workforce—or do more with the same workforce—the future economics of the business could become more cost-competitive and possibly lead to higher margins.

Risk Reduction   Many enterprise buyers also want reduce the overall risk profile of their business—for example, by helping minimize the potential for cyberattacks, product theft, safety incidents, brand damage, and more. The Tylenol tampering case of the 1980s is a good example of a company whose brand was severely damaged by the fallout from the incident that led to several deaths. Although the manufacturer Johnson & Johnson quickly came up with a tamper-proof bottle, the damage was already done and it took years for the brand to recover. Imagine the value of a proactive investment in tamper-proof years before the incident.

An investment in corporate risk reduction can translate into significant business value for B2B companies. For example, Gartner (www.gartner.com/en/insights) calculates that for each minute of IT network downtime, the average business loses $5,600.[2] That amounts to losses of over $300,000 per hour for a large company. Clearly, avoiding such downtime would generate a positive ROI, as would a smart investment in reducing cyber-related risks such as a data breach or ransomware attack that could derail business operations for days, weeks, or longer.

---

[2] www.gartner.com/en/insights.

Financial Impact   The PMO-managed purchase process will likely include an executive-level assessment of the overall financial impact of the investment. The business will want to understand the total investment required (OpEx and CapEx), timing of the investment, time to production and market, and how quickly it will realize financial benefits—such as revenue increases and cost reductions. Other common KPIs such as payback period, internal rate of return, and total net present value of financial benefit will be part of this assessment.

Building a Value-Based Narrative: The Business Case

When a major financial investment is at stake, buyers will often ask the vendors to submit a formal business case to better understand the business value of the proposed solution and to help secure funding. The business case justifies the investment by laying out its benefits, costs, and risks, and showing how it aligns with the company's strategic business objectives. Often, the goal of the business case is to convince the customer's investment committee that the product or service will deliver one or more of these critical business outcomes:

- Grow the business (revenue growth)
- Run the business (improved OpEx)
- Protect the business (less enterprise risk)

There are almost always more investment ideas than the supply of capital available to fund them. Options abound, so when it comes to technology investments, companies may want to compare an IT-centric purchase with other investment ideas. For example, retailers may weigh investing in a point-of-service technology system versus opening a new store; a manufacturer may consider buying new technologies to modernize its manufacturing line versus developing a brand new product. The business case thus provides an *investment thesis* that allows decision-makers to make the best choice among rival investment opportunities.

Three Phases in Building a Business Case

There are typically three phases to building a business case:

Phase 1: Value Discovery   This critical step aims at understanding the customer's current operational objectives, strategic objectives, financial objectives, risk challenges, and other customer needs that influence the product or solution positioning.

Phase 2: Value Analysis   Next, the vendor maps its product capabilities to the customer's unique set of business challenges. The analysis drills into the current business processes and determines how they will be improved by implementing the company's proposed offering. At this stage, it's important to differentiate hard savings from soft savings. This raises the question of whether the savings will drive a measurable impact on the income statement or simply improve a process that may save time without reducing the resources needed to complete a task.

Phase 3: Value Synthesis   Finally, the authors of the business case pull together data from the previous steps to create summary reports to be reviewed and validated by the customer's executive decision-makers. The summaries should be presented individually to each stakeholder and designed to forge a strong consensus for approving the investment and actively advocating for funding the project.

When done properly, a good business case helps both sellers and buyers achieve their objectives:

- Sellers win more deals when they create a good business case and then demonstrate that they can deliver on the promised value; this builds trust and customer loyalty and ultimately maximizes customer lifetime value.
- Project sponsors on the buyer side can justify their preferred investment versus other options when seeking approval from C-level executives and board members.

Note that the business case, while an essential asset in closing a deal, represents only one step in the customer's journey, but for many companies this is where most value management programs begin. Table 2.2 shows some key tips for building a great business case.

Table 2.2: Helpful hints for building a business case

WHAT TO DISCOVER	QUESTIONS TO ASK THE CUSTOMER:	IDENTIFY WHO PARTICIPATES	HOW AND WHEN IS THIS DONE?
Business Objectives	Company-level (or enterprise)	Senior customer executives across all the VP-level functions	Discovery phase > Research and Interviews
	■ What is the customer's enterprise mission and vision?		1 week
	■ What are the industry's notable trends and priorities?	Influencers/users (director/ manager/ individual contributors)	
	■ What are the customer's enterprise business objectives and goals? Specify strategic, financial, customer and employee, and Environmental, Social, and Governance (ESG) objectives and goals.		
	■ What are their strategies/initiatives to achieve those objectives?		
	Function-level (or process)		
	■ What is the function's mission and vision?		
	■ What are the function's business objectives and goals? Specify strategic, financial, customer and employee, and ESG objectives and goals.		
	■ What are their strategies/initiatives to achieve those objectives?		
	Individual-level (or role)		
	■ What are the individual's business objectives and goals? Specify strategic, financial, customer and employee, and ESG objectives and goals.		
	■ What are their strategies/initiatives to achieve those objectives?		
	At all three levels: If you had to ask only one question, it would be "What are you solving for?"		

WHAT TO DISCOVER		
QUESTIONS TO ASK THE CUSTOMER:	**IDENTIFY WHO PARTICIPATES**	**HOW AND WHEN IS THIS DONE?**
Techniques to get this information: In-depth interview prompts: ■ We need a … ■ We want to … ■ We have a challenge with … ■ We need better … ■ We need to make sure … ■ We want to improve … Document research: "Please share any latest presentations or documents from which I can understand these." ■ Internet research ■ 10k reports ■ Google Search ■ APQC (American Productivity & Quality Center) ■ Databook ■ Consulting websites		

Continues

Table 2.2: *(Continued)*

WHAT TO DISCOVER	QUESTIONS TO ASK THE CUSTOMER:	IDENTIFY WHO PARTICIPATES	HOW AND WHEN IS THIS DONE?
Challenges/ Opportunities	■ What challenges prevent them from achieving these objectives? ■ What are the opportunities that need to be converted? Document research "Please share any latest presentations or documents from which I can understand these."	Customer executives across all the functions VP-level and director-level	Discovery phase > Research and Interviews 1 week
Capabilities/ Solution	■ What business capabilities would the customer need to acquire or enhance in order to overcome these challenges/convert the opportunities? ■ Which of these capabilities is the customer looking to acquire/enhance in the current initiative? ■ What solution will bring these capabilities together to overcome challenges and achieve the objectives? ■ What is the technology solution proposed by the vendor? (done by Solution Consultant) ■ What is the business process and technology architecture of the proposed solution? (done by Solution Consultant) ■ What is the total investment required? (done by Account Executive) ■ Which are the functions and business processes (or use cases) that will be most impacted by this solution? ("the Before") ■ What features of the vendor's product will provide the capabilities required? ■ With these features, how will the impacted functions and business processes (or use cases) work after the solution is implemented?	Customer executives across all the functions; director-level and some users Review with VP level	Analysis phase 2 weeks

WHAT TO DISCOVER	QUESTIONS TO ASK THE CUSTOMER:	IDENTIFY WHO PARTICIPATES	HOW AND WHEN IS THIS DONE?
Outcomes	■ What are the quantifiable and qualitative outcomes that will be achieved when the solution is implemented?	Customer executives across all the functions; director-level and some users	Synthesis
	■ What are the key metrics related to each use case that will improve?		2 weeks
	■ What benefits can the enterprise, each function, leadership personas, and user personas expect?		
	■ What is the ROI, NPV, IRR, and payback of the overall investment?	Review with VP level	
	■ Summarize the strategic and financial whys of the vendor's proposed solution, i.e., how it is aligned to the customer's business objectives and strategies; contrast the "Before" with "After" business processes; what quantifiable and qualitative outcomes can be expected.		

DEFINING A GOOD BUSINESS CASE

Here's what to look for in a good business case:

- It articulates the enterprise business value, outcomes, and ROI that will be achieved, and does so in a clear, compelling, and credible manner.

- It describes both the quantitative and qualitative benefits to the enterprise, function, and stakeholder personas.

- It defines a "road map to value"—that is, what activities need to be performed to realize the expected value.

- It explains why the proposed investment is essential versus a nice-to-have by showing how it will support or complement the customer's business strategies and help achieve the customer's business objectives.

- It compares how work will be done after the solution is implemented versus how work is done today.

- It communicates all the above with clarity and conviction so that the primary budget owner in the customer's organization can enthusiastically "own the business case" and advocate for it internally to secure funds.

A Simple Home Purchase Example: Solar Panels

To get a feel for a simple case study, here's an example of one that you may have faced in your household: investing in home solar. It's fairly easy to compare the total costs of installing and operating solar panels with the costs and savings of moving to solar power. Table 2.3 presents a simple illustration.

Table 2.3   The business value of solar

COST OF TRADITIONAL POWER	
Current cost of power provided by the electric company	$0.20 per kWh
Average monthly consumption of power in my house	500 kWh
Current monthly cost of power	$100
Annual cost of power	$1,200
10-year cost of power	$12,000

COST OF TRADITIONAL POWER	
Cost and power savings from solar panels	
Estimated investment in solar panels for my house	$5,400, one time
Cost of solar power	$0 per kWh $100
Electricity company fees for connecting to the power grid for any extra power required	$20 per month
Annual cost of solar power	$240
10-Year cost of solar power	**$7,800** ($2,400 over 10 years plus the one-time investment of $5,400) A **35%** savings over our current system

Of course, this is an oversimplified analysis of the overall cost savings over 10 years from deploying solar panels. In the real world, there are many other factors to consider, such as the future rates of traditional power, upkeep and maintenance for solar panels, and risks related to damage from natural weather events such as hail. Yet, this straightforward analysis of the two alternatives provides a simple glimpse of what a value engineer would present to the homeowner interested in solar power to help them make an informed decision on the investment.

Beyond Case Studies

Although creating a great business case is one of the most important skills you can learn as part of your value management effort, it's important to put it in a broader framework and think of case studies as a *single-point-in-time activity* that you engage in periodically across a multiyear customer life cycle, starting with solution awareness and ending with value realization and expansion.

Let's dig deeper into the ways that value management tasks and activities can be integrated into the customer life cycle and explain why some companies get stuck when trying to scale out their programs. We'll review how companies have traditionally organized their value management teams and the limitations and pitfalls they've run into along the way. The current state of value management discussed in this chapter will form the basis for how we define the *future state* of value management powered by AI, which we'll explore in subsequent chapters.

Understanding the Customer Life Cycle

Throughout the customer life cycle, multiple business teams (functions) play important roles in successfully moving the customer from one stage to the next (see Figure 2.1). Ideally, the transitions are smooth, but there are plenty of opportunities to drop the ball if there is confusion or miscommunications between teams. We've seen more than a few companies struggle to synchronize value management messaging, coordinate handoffs, and orchestrate a holistic technology strategy, leading to an inconsistent and bumpy customer experience and even lost sales.

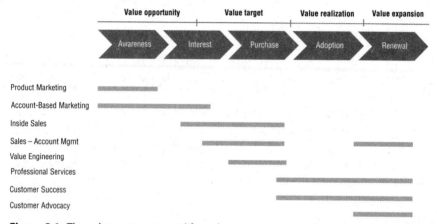

Figure 2.1: The value management life cycle

For example, when a customer takes an interest in a product, they often start by visiting the vendor's website, which may advertise all kinds of great features and promise exciting business benefits. But the customer may discover later that the actual benefits are likely to be much less valuable. This can create trust issues that sales teams must overcome to close the sale, increasing the time to close a deal and potentially putting the deal in jeopardy.

Go-to-Market Collaboration: The Key to Value Management Success

A successful value management program requires close collaboration across multiple business functions, including sales, marketing, customer success, professional services, and executive teams. Each team member needs to be versed on the latest value-related conversations with the customer and be familiar with the expectations set during these discussions. Teams should then build on the trust established during these early interactions by working to ensure the customer achieves their desired business outcomes.

Here are some of the typical roles and responsibilities of a B2B company's value management team:

- **Account Executive** has overall ownership of the customer relationship and is responsible for meeting their sales quota for new and renewal contracts.

- **Solution Consultant, Pre-Sales Consultant, and Enterprise Architects** are responsible for proposing the technology solution to the customer, as well as conducting demos. This role may also be referred to as Sales Engineers and Solution Sales Executives.

- **Value Management and Value Engineering Consultants** are responsible for developing the financial modeling of the company's products and creating the business case to support the sales opportunity. Often, the value engineers also help with executive briefings and workshops to deepen the customer relationship.

- **Professional Services** teams deploy the solution for the customer. These teams support the financial modeling effort by providing the value engineer with the implementation timeline and associated fees that detail timing of benefits and costs related to the project.

- **Customer Success Managers** work with existing customers to drive product usage, accelerate the adoption maturity at the customer, and maximize the value realized from the company's solutions. These resources are critical to successful renewal and expansion for existing customers by providing solution road maps and complementary products and services to build on past deployments.

- **Customer Advocacy Representatives** are typically marketing resources that help the company recruit and nurture customer references, manage customer advisory boards, and deliver marketing content for events, conferences, and executive briefings that showcase past customer success stories.

- **Product Marketing Managers** are responsible for creating marketing and sales content, driving product positioning, value modeling and pricing decisions, and managing promotional activities to spread awareness for the company's products and services.

- **Partner Sales Teams** help companies scale their sales effort by adding resources to support smaller customers, cover international markets, or provide complementary products and services to expand sales opportunities.

As you might imagine, with so many people needing to work together, companies can struggle to present a unified front throughout the customer life cycle. Inconsistent messaging, stop-and-start value management activities, and inaccurate or overinflated promises can slow or even derail the buying process.[3]

A common problem B2B companies run into is when an overly ambitious marketing group advertises inflated benefits that are inconsistent with the more conservative ROI business case. The problem can be compounded when the business case itself doesn't reflect the parameters of the final sales deal, a disconnect that can delay or diminish realization of the business value initially promised. With so many internal teams and outside partners interacting with the customer throughout the life cycle, B2B sellers would do well to need to invest in building a well-structured and scalable value messaging platform for each of their solutions.

Solution Value Messaging

The objective of a solution value messaging platform is to translate your product's capabilities (features and functions) into business benefits in a language that the customer can understand. The resulting value messaging provides customers with a detailed and defensible view of the business outcomes they can anticipate when they invest in one or more of the company's solutions. Ideally, the solution messaging platform will "map" each element of the solution to its corresponding value potential and explains how these business outcomes can be achieved.

---

[3]It's no surprise that customers expect the company they're dealing with to speak with a single voice. That's why it's critical for companies to ensure accurate and consistent *value messaging* across the customer life cycle or risk losing the trust of the customer right at the beginning of the sales cycle.

VALUE MESSAGING PLATFORM

Typical elements of a solution value messaging platform include:

- ▪ "Value trees" that map product features and capabilities to its expected business outcomes

- ▪ ROI worksheets that help calculate the customer's business value potential

- ▪ Key business metrics that represent value, such as ROI, IRR, NPV, and payback period

---

Value Models

Product managers and value engineers will often develop a value model that represents, in a structured form, the range of product features, their unique capabilities, and potential business outcomes with their associated KPIs. In our client projects, we often use a "value tree" to build these value models. Ideally, a value model forms the basis for all marketing and sales content related to the product's go-to-market activities. The model can be used to develop interview guides for customer success stories, business case data collection, lead-gen tools, customer success tools, and more.

Since the "value tree" is set in the early days of the customer life cycle, let's dig deeper into the initial Value Opportunity phase.

The Value Opportunity Stage (Awareness + Interest)

Today, most customers do their initial product research on the Internet. Using online searches, they can identify the highest potential solutions and then reduce the field to a handful of qualified vendors. Thus, in this early Value Opportunity stage, most of the information gathering happens without human interactions. Indeed, most modern marketing-automation systems use sophisticated prospect-scoring techniques to create optimized "nurturing paths" to determine when prospects are deemed "ready" for direct communications (see Figure 2.2).

During this early phase, companies deploy specialized teams—namely, *product marketing, account-based marketing*, and *inside sales* teams—to make sure their demand generation campaigns, digital content, and other marketing and sales tools connect with potential prospects and generate qualified leads to maximize the sales pipeline.

Figure 2.2: The Value Opportunity stage

In our experience, Value Opportunity teams/programs can have mixed results. Smaller companies, such as startups, may find better success simply because coordinating marketing teams is easier at that scale and product portfolios are less complex. But as companies grow and their products and services proliferate, these teams can easily become disconnected and lose focus and effectiveness. As a result, demand-generation campaigns can lack clear, value-oriented messaging; customer needs can be misunderstood; and leads can be mis-scored and not followed up properly.

Handoffs from inside sales to enterprise sales teams can be even more problematic. Creating a sales-qualified lead record can be fraught with errors. Prospect conversations might lack important details or fail to demonstrate domain or industry knowledge, leaving the customer with a bad impression of the company.

Chapter 4, "AI-Driven Value Management for Marketing," discusses these challenges in detail and explores how a modern value management program powered by AI can overcome these challenges and drive the first of our "2-to-the-power-of-3" customer outcomes: 2X lead generation.

FROM AWARENESS TO INTEREST

Budding sales opportunities are nurtured in a three-stage process:

1. **Lead:** Potential customers (leads) are identified.

2. **Prospect:** After initial contact, if a lead shows interest, they are often moved to the "prospect" stage. Your sales team works to learn more about the prospect's needs and how their offering can meet these needs.

3. **Qualification:** This stage involves evaluating whether a prospect has a genuine need for your product or service, have the budget for it, and can authorize a purchase.

VM PRO TIP

To present a unified voice to the customer, your value management program should follow a single playbook to make sure each team delivers a consistent value-based message and avoids confusing signals that can undermine customer trust.

The Value Target Stage (Interest + Purchase)

After prospects have been sufficiently vetted and meet the requirements of a promising "sales-qualified lead," the next steps are significantly more labor-intensive. Typically, this Value Target stage (see Figure 2.3) is managed by a designated sales account executive with the help of an extended sales team that could include solution consultants, enterprise architects, and business value consultants. These resources bring deep, firsthand knowledge of the industry, existing customer relationships, solution acumen, and technical expertise. Together they ensure that the prospect's key decision-makers are satisfied that the company and its products meet their specific needs.

Figure 2.3: The Value Target stage

This multifunctional team now leads the engagement from the *interest* phase to the *purchase* phase of the sales cycle. This process can take weeks or even months to play out. To coordinate and record the activities of multiple salespeople and a number of buyer-side decision-makers, the help of a customer resource management (CRM) system is often required, with Salesforce being a leading example.

The Value Target stage is where value management programs typically find their first "home." Business value consultants, for example, usually supply the thought leadership presented at executive customer briefings and build sophisticated economic models used to develop business cases. These consultants also work closely with customers to create an "investment thesis," which they present it to the customers' top executives.

During this phase, sales account teams typically play the role of a general contractor, coordinating meetings with customer decision-makers, helping teams identify the scope of the deal, negotiating the deal's terms and conditions, and managing the contracting process. Professional services teams (internal or system implementation partners)—which are tasked with installing the solutions—are brought in to create the "statement of work," which sets the timeline for the different phases of product implementation and estimates budget requirements.

This stage of the value management process can be tricky. On the front end, the handoff from lead generators to sales teams and business value consultants can be murky at best. Often there's a lack of background information on the prospect's recent activity related to the opportunity, such as what materials they've consumed, what communications they've shared, and prior understandings of their unique needs. This can be frustrating for the customer, who may need to regurgitate earlier conversations.

There are other challenges: On the back end, after the sale has closed, many sales teams and business value consultants have moved on to the next sales opportunity. Since commissions often represent a major part of their compensation, many are tempted to "bag and bolt." However, in today's subscription-based, customer-first economy, this is a mistake. The Value Realization phase is core to ensuring a successful long-term relationship with the customer and maintaining ongoing revenue streams based on successful product renewals.

The Value Realization Stage (Adoption)

It's done—the deal is closed! This is where the Value Realization stage (see Figure 2.4) begins and when customers—if all goes well—can finally reap the rewards of their investment. A professional services team (sometimes partners are hired) usually kicks off this phase, overseeing the implementation of the newly acquired products and services. For large enterprise solutions—think of a global computer network—this can be a huge effort, taking months, if not years, to complete. Yet the technical deployment of the system isn't necessarily the hardest part. Even tougher is ensuring that people *adopt* the solution and that the customer achieves the business outcomes it was promised.

Figure 2.4: The Value Realization stage

That can leave the professional services team in an awkward position as it tries to balance the expectations of the customer—often fueled by the lofty vision of the original business case—with the down-to-earth realities and constraints of the final negotiated budget (or statement of work). Indeed, these last-minute refinements in project scope and budget can lead to disappointment and distrust just when the customer relationship is gaining traction.

We've seen it happen many times before. Recently, for example, we saw a multibillion-dollar telecom company greenlight a new CRM system for its employees and customers. The vendor's value consultant/engineer who helped sell the investment put together a detailed "value tree" (a detailed list of quantified business-value drivers) for the telco's board of directors. After the board approved the project, the systems implementer (SI), working with the CRM provider, developed an acceptable initial project scope and statement of work. But that was followed by a slew of revisions and refinements. Fast-forward 18 months later: The board's expectations of big performance gains never materialized, thanks to the subsequent rounds of scoping and design changes. The project was put on hold indefinitely and the relationship between the CRM vendor and its SI was never the same.

After the implementation phase is complete and the solution is up and running, it's time for the company's *customer success team* to take over responsibility for value management, encouraging employees to use the product and explore its potential, and pushing the business to leverage the investment more broadly, ultimately ensuring value creation throughout the length of the contract (or subscription) period.

Speed bumps can lurk here as well. Customer success teams need to be alert to any changes that happened during the implementation phase of the solution, as well as any gaps (mentioned previously) between the initial business case and the final statement of work. Ignoring these issues can lead to miscommunications around the perceived success of the deployment and the business outcomes achieved.

The Value Expansion Stage (Renewal)

Customers will eventually reach the end of their subscription period or product life cycle. Well-executed value management programs—powered by AI—can help companies renew and extend the value proposition for their customers and achieve expanded business outcomes in the process.

We're now entering the Value Expansion stage (see Figure 2.5). That's when the contract, subscription, or licensing agreement has ended. For many companies, if their products and services matched or beat their customer's expectations, getting them to renew can be a simple layup and takes minimal sales effort. Indeed, most companies are content with this steady-state scenario; account teams draft up the renewal agreement and assume the customer will sign it. Little or no communication with the customer is needed or desired.

Figure 2.5: The Value Expansion stage

A value management approach argues for a different strategy. For forward-thinking companies that embrace this concept, subscription and contract renewals offer an incredible opportunity for expanding sales and deepening customer loyalty. Smart sales and value engineering/management teams that *get it* will look at this point in the life cycle as a prime expansion opportunity within the account.

Seizing this opportunity is often the work of *sales account teams* with the support of *customer success* and *value engineering* teams. The teams may promote complementary solutions that add to or enhance the customer's current footprint. *Customer advocacy teams*—typically part of the marketing department—can also play a valuable role at this point in the sales cycle. For example, they'll ask the company's largest or most strategic *customer advocates* to join customer advisory boards to share best practices and build a community of users and product enthusiasts. Customer advocacy teams also secure customer references to help build powerful first-person marketing content, support demand-gen programs, and provide proof-points of business outcomes.

VM PRO TIP

Marketing-based customer advocacy teams are a great resource to capture customer success stories and best-practice insights, creating a feedback loop that continually improves your company's overall value proposition.

There are numerous functional teams required across each of the value stages to effectively pursue an end-to-end value management program. Each stage has a set of capabilities, coverage, and customer outcomes that need to be defined, structured, and executed to deliver on the full promise of 2-to-the-power-of-3 customer outcomes.

In the next chapter, we'll lay out how we see artificial intelligence as a technology breakthrough to remove the current barriers facing these programs.

Building the Future Value Management Program

Chapter 2, "The Current State of Value Management," charted the end-to-end scope of value management programs/practices and their impact on the customer life cycle. We also looked at the multifunctional organizational roles and responsibilities that must work collaboratively to fully enable a value management program. Despite the challenges of scaling value management programs, the future of value management powered by AI is within reach, offering B2B companies practical strategies and tools to unlock revenue at scale.

The Game Changer: Artificial Intelligence

When generative AI (GenAI) broke into the public consciousness in 2023, it amazed ordinary users and caught the eye of the business world with its ability to self-generate new content such as images, text, or music. It was clear we had come a long way from rule-based algorithms that characterized AI in the 1950s to the 1980s and the neural networks of the 1980s and '90s (see Figure 3.1). The early 2000s saw rapid developments in predictive AI and machine learning (ML) with the availability of computing power at dramatically lower costs.

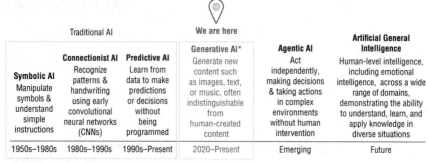

Symbolic AI	Connectionist AI	Predictive AI	Generative AI*	Agentic AI	Artificial General Intelligence
	Traditional AI		We are here		
Manipulate symbols & understand simple instructions	Recognize patterns & handwriting using early convolutional neural networks (CNNs)	Learn from data to make predictions or decisions without being programmed	Generate new content such as images, text, or music, often indistinguishable from human-created content	Act independently, making decisions & taking actions in complex environments without human intervention	Human-level intelligence, including emotional intelligence, across a wide range of domains, demonstrating the ability to understand, learn, and apply knowledge in diverse situations
1950s–1980s	1980s–1990s	1990s–Present	2020–Present	Emerging	Future

*Not all AI is not GenAI, but all GenAI is AI.

Figure 3.1: AI's rapidly evolving landscape

AI: Past, Present, and Future

GenAI is just getting started and there are many more innovations on the horizon. For example, agentic AI (also known as autonomous AI) is rapidly being developed and holds more potential for businesses beyond GenAI. Agentic AI can act independently, making decisions and taking actions in complex environments without human intervention.

These emerging AI capabilities offer an answer to the question of how to scale value management and multiply its impact throughout the business. We believe that currently, a combination of predictive AI and GenAI will offer a new blueprint for an AI-driven value management blueprint. They will complement an array of already deployed enterprise SaaS solutions—from advanced cloud applications to data cloud platforms.

COMPLEMENTARY VALUE MANAGEMENT TECHNOLOGIES

GenAI, complemented by other technological advancements, will overcome today's barriers to scaling value management programs. These complementary solutions include:

- **Advanced SaaS applications** can digitize work with best-of-breed workflows and tools for marketing, sales, and customer success.

- **Advanced analytics and data science insights** from large language models (LLMs) and data lakes can be used to forecast, track, and measure how customers use their products and benefit from their capabilities.

- **New value-automation SaaS platforms** can provide fast, standardized ways to model, quantify, and communicate benefits, ROI business cases, and realized outcomes to their sales and customer success teams and their customers.

Think of AI as the engine behind a new technology platform designed to scale value management without the enormous labor expense and overhead that has slowed advancement of current value management leaders. Even for the most advanced value management practitioner, AI will unlock massive new potential from existing value management investments.

AI-VM: Competitive Advantage at Scale

We can now begin to lay out an AI-driven value management approach that will help you create a competitive advantage at an unprecedented scale. We will look at real-world use cases from companies such as Salesforce, Amazon Web Services (AWS), Google, Hewlett Packard Enterprise (HPE), ServiceNow, SAP, and Oracle. Then we will combine that with the potential of new AI capabilities to explain how businesses can orchestrate people, processes, and technologies to build what we call the value management solution of the future: an *AI-powered value management program*—or AI-VM.

We will also look at the challenges these companies faced in scaling their value management program without AI and highlight where and how you can use AI to avoid those pitfalls. We will feature a detailed breakdown of use cases for GenAI and the latest tools and integrations to easily and cost-effectively architect and roll out their AI-VM programs.

Let's start by looking at the different AI capabilities that can be harnessed to enhance current value management practices:

Level 1—GenAI Out-of-the-Box   Currently, this is the most accessible form of AI for enterprises, offering AI-enabled content generation and conversational search capabilities. OpenAI's ChatGPT and Google Gemini are just two of the many examples out there today. However, the ability to measure adoption and business value outcomes can be difficult given the novelty of the solutions and the opacity of business use cases.

Example: Automatically summarize customer meeting notes, action items, and key questions.

Level 2—GenAI with Extensive Prompt Engineering   With retrieval augmented generation and predictive AI techniques, specific business problems can be solved more effectively.

Example: A salesperson can ask questions about a customer's financial performance and the GenAI solution provides insightful answers from a company's public financial reports (e.g., 10-K / 10-Q SEC Reports).

Level 3—Functional Workflows with GenAI + Predictive AI   Custom-built applications with AI content and conversational Q&A features are integrated with other existing business applications to create a new level of digitized, automated functional workflows. Companies have the potential to throw away existing business practices and redesign legacy functional workflows to make the most of AI automation.

Example: Identify sales opportunities that need specific recourse at each stage of a deal's sales cycle; e.g., a customer reads a solution whitepaper and needs more specific details about its impact to their industry.

Level 4—Enterprise Workflows with GenAI + Predictive AI   Custom-built applications with solutions that span multiple functional workflows. New multifunction workflows can unlock significant value for the business.

Example: Automatically tracking the status of a qualified customer—from lead generation and other marketing activities—to pre-sales engagement, post-sales adoption, and renewal activity. Customers can be positioned to increase wallet share via cross-sell and up-sell opportunities.

Introducing a Blueprint for AI-Value Management

Creating an enterprise-level value management capability can be challenging, and many of the best global companies struggle to scale their programs today. Think of the early days of the Internet and the challenges industry leaders had before the digital revolution. We lived through it—it wasn't solved overnight. Many of the high-octane startups of the day—AOL, Netscape, Webvan—quickly flamed out, and the same can happen to organizations that do not build their value management programs effectively using the full potential of AI. In our view, AI presents a new platform by which value management can be built on top of. However, the blueprint for value management is much more than just technology—it requires a full view of the people, process, and technology components necessary for success.

To help companies capture the new AI-VM opportunity, we created a simple framework that brings together three critical elements: *building capabilities, expanding coverage,* and *realizing customer success.* All three are closely related in cause and effect. When you have the right capabilities and comprehensive coverage, you are primed to maximize customer success. This unified framework will underpin the approach to building the next-generation AI-VM programs and achieve 2-to-the-power-of-3 business outcomes.

Let's take a closer look at the elements of the framework:

- **AI-VM capabilities**—People, process, technology, organizational design, governance, and other management constructs, powered by AI:

  - The *People* element explores aspects such as team size, skill sets, and headcount ratios for account executives, solution consultants, value management consultants, customer success managers, and leadership.

  - The *Process* element defines specific requirements for executing value management at scale, such as value taxonomy, workflows, methodology, services, customer and internal engagement, operating models, and qualification criteria.

  - The *Technology & AI* element specifies what types of applications, tools, and platforms are required at various stages. This includes CRM systems, value automation tools, analytics, and AI assistants.

  - The *Organization* element explores the right structure for the optimal impact—specifically, where the value management organization should be placed and its reporting structure.

  - The *Governance* element defines how the program will be governed for success, including defining key performance indicators for monitoring the program.

  - The *Planning* element lays out a process for forecasting the company's needs for value management resources (people, tools, and services) and the outcomes (pipeline, revenue, and expansion) that can be expected as a result. This is an annual exercise that involves making the business case for value management resources and budgets.

- The *Community* element involves bringing everyone who practices value management—whether from Marketing, Product, Sales, or Customer Success—into one value community for sharing of thought leadership and best practices.

- **AI-VM coverage**—Coverage looks at the operational scope in which the value management program is being executed; these include:

  - The *Solutions* element, especially for large enterprise companies, structures the approach to deploying value management across the portfolio of products/services that the company provides.

  - The *Customer Segments* element defines which customers are covered by the value management program. This can be industry, size, or solution specific.

  - The *Customer Opportunities* element determines which deals are covered by the value management program. Decisions can be made by constructs such as deal size, strategic impact, and customer lifetime value.

  - The *Geographies* element structures how value management is deployed across organizational geographic units.

  - The *Channel/Partners* element defines how the program is extended to the channel and includes partner sales organizations in delivering value management capabilities.

- **AI-VM customer success**—Identifies the company business results, or key performance indicators, that provide economic and strategic impact of the value management program:

  - The *Sales Pipeline* element measures the increases to the sales funnel driven by value management practices.

  - The *Revenue Growth* element measures increased revenue driven by VM practices.

  - The *Win Rates* element measures increased percentages of successful deals that are impacted by VM practices.

  - The *Churn Rates* element measures the increase in successful renewals of existing customers driven by VM practices.

  - The *Share of Wallet* element measures increases in revenue per customer driven by VM practices.

- The *Customer Satisfaction* element measures improved customer satisfaction rates driven by VM practices.

- The *Deal Margin* element measures increases in margin contribution driven by VM practices.

We will refer to this framework in the following chapters to help you better understand the powerful synergies between AI-VM capabilities, coverage, and customer success. In the process, we will define the future state of value management across four stages: Value Opportunity, Value Target, Value Realization, and Value Expansion. We will start with the Value Target stage because this is typically where value management begins. Many companies start with the hiring of a single business value consultant (or value engineer) to work on a few strategic deals. The success of that pilot leads to opportunities to scale to a full value management program.

4

AI-Driven Value Management for Marketing

What's the connection between marketing and value management? Think of it this way: If marketing is about telling great stories, what is more impactful than telling the story about the business value you can provide to your customers? In fact, you could even say that marketing and value management were meant for each other. However, although there are obvious synergies, even useful content that connects the two, there is a scarcity of proven methods and techniques that help companies profit from a comprehensive value management capability for marketing.

This chapter looks at three types of marketing you will find in any enterprise B2B company today: product marketing, revenue marketing, and corporate marketing (see Figure 4.1). We'll look at how leading companies run B2B marketing today, and then lay out the future state of B2B marketing powered by AI-driven value management (AI-VM) solutions for marketing. We will highlight leading marketing programs and how they plan to integrate value management concepts and generative AI to supercharge their go-to-market content, lead generation programs, and brand equity impacts. We also will focus our discussion on areas in marketing that can benefit by deploying AI-VM capabilities.

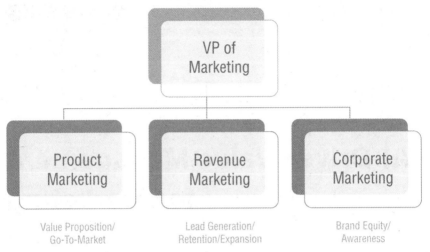

Figure 4.1: B2B marketing organizational structure

Empowering B2B Marketing with AI-Enabled Value Management

Simply put, product marketing, revenue marketing, and corporate marketing all aim to create awareness for the company's offerings and generate leads and pipeline. But the connection between marketing activities and pipeline remains hard to establish and often isn't tailored to the specific expectations of the audience. That's why marketers will be the first to tell you that marketing ROI is still difficult to prove.

If marketing initiatives were focused on business outcomes that matter to individual customers (or segments), marketing teams could better measure the impact of these initiatives. For example, to market new technology innovations to an enterprise-scale grocery retailer, a tech company needed to prove that its solution would improve store operating margins. Instead of focusing on traditional technology metrics such as MIPS,[1] data storage capacity, and bandwidth, the company's marketing team focused on what matters to the business: reduced merchandise shrinkage, lower IT costs, and an optimized store footprint.

That is the essence of a marketing approach called *account-based marketing (ABM)*.[2] The approach has been gaining in popularity over

---

[1] MIPS, which stands for Microprocessor without Interlocked Pipelined Stages, is a measurement of a computer's processing speed.

[2] Account-based marketing (ABM) is a growth strategy where marketing and sales work together to target key accounts that showcase significant revenue opportunities. Companies utilize B2B data to create highly personalized marketing campaigns and buyer experiences for each account. Source: www.cognism.com/blog/account-based-marketing.

the past two decades, with two-thirds of companies now implementing some form of ABM.[3] However, this promising marketing strategy has been held back by several factors, including:

- The lack of easy access to relevant customer insights
- Poor collaboration between sales and marketing teams
- Limited integration across marketing and sales processes
- Slow adoption of underlying automation technologies

It is by overcoming these hurdles that AI can lend a big helping hand. In this book, our focus will be on how a next-gen ABM strategy powered by AI can help value management programs reach their maximum potential. This new and improved ABM program will be transformational compared to how it operates in B2B enterprises today and destined to be the dominant operating model for sales and marketing organizations in the years ahead.

A PROFESSOR'S PREDICTION PROVES PRESCIENT

When Craig was in business school in the mid-'90s, he was fortunate to take a course with Dr. Rohit Deshpande, one of the world's leading marketing professors (and currently a professor at Harvard Business School). In one of his classes, he remembers Dr. Deshpande making a profound prediction: "Someone, someday will figure out how to measure the ROI impact of marketing programs and when they do, they will make a fortune." Sure enough, a decade later, along came Google Ads, social media, and marketing automation solutions like Marketo and HubSpot, yielding a stream of profits for these companies and their customers. Dr. Deshpande's prediction had finally become a reality. Still, the search continues for new technologies that will help businesses get even more out of their marketing dollar. Craig is confident AI and value management will play a lead role in this next chapter of the B2B marketing revolution.

The Current State of B2B Marketing

In the last decade or so, B2B marketing has undergone a complete makeover, with digital and multimedia channels and self-service product research via the web now dominating the landscape. Research by Gartner

---

[3] "B2B Account-Based Marketing Statistics for 2024," Lauren O'Brien, April 2024 (https://www.poweredbysearch.com/learn/b2b-abm-statistics).

Inc. determined that "80% of B2B sales interactions between suppliers and buyers will occur in digital channels."[4] The skills of marketers today have changed as well, with increasing specialization in areas such as digital marketing, data analytics, hybrid event management, and digital demand generation.

Even with all the modernizations that B2B marketing has implemented, there remains large barriers to overcome. To stay competitive, modern marketers need to coordinate even more effectively with other parts of the organization, such as sales, customer success, and professional services. This is particularly important for value management because its ability to gather *value intelligence* is critical to maximizing sales results. Simply put, value intelligence is marketing content containing business insights and key performance indicators (KPIs) that prove how the company's products and services can deliver positive ROI for customers. Unfortunately, B2B marketing teams typically don't have the expertise to capture relevant value intelligence for their companies.

Without this domain expertise, it's difficult for these teams to effectively partner with other functions that are critical to developing value intelligence. Some companies may redeploy value management resources to help out, but that can lead to high costs and spark turf battles between value engineering and marketing teams. In truth, this is just a "Band-Aid" approach.

Let's look at where B2B marketing stands today across each of our three areas of focus: product marketing, revenue marketing, and corporate marketing.

Product Marketing: Account-Based Marketing Barriers to Scale

Product marketing is typically one of the largest marketing teams in B2B enterprises. Responsible for developing the product's go-to-market plans, these teams identify the best markets and buyers to go after. Their goal: Increase sales by generating greater awareness of the product and accelerating the customer journey, ultimately leading to increased revenues via higher win rates and a bigger market share.

What role can value management play in product marketing? The idea of integrating value management and marketing is still new, and

---

[4] Source: https://www.gartner.com/en/newsroom/press-releases/ 2020-09-15-gartner-says-80--of-b2b-sales-interactions- between-su.

most B2B companies are still experimenting with what works best. While we see some product marketers diligently developing *value messaging*, rarely do they have access to the same direct lines of communications to customers that frontline value engineering or sales teams enjoy. That makes it hard for marketers to reality-check their product positioning and develop credible KPIs and benchmarks. Plus, it can be difficult to keep content up to date when feedback from sales and customer success teams is not freely shared with them.

Indeed, perhaps the biggest hurdle facing revenue marketers today is the lack of collaboration with sales teams. A recent study by the cloud marketing company Intricately (recently acquired by HG Insights) found that "50% of the B2B companies surveyed said their sales and marketing teams do not collaborate in revenue GTM programs."[5]

This gap will only become more glaring as B2B companies attempt to create content for their ABM programs. The disconnect was evident at a leading global SaaS company we studied, where a value engineering team in the sales organization wanted to share detailed business cases with the product marketing teams to help create ROI customer case studies. But between translating detailed cash flow models and deciphering cryptic management consulting lingo, the marketers gave up in frustration—and the valuable market data was left unused.

BRINGING VALUE INTELLIGENCE INTO MARKETING: IT'S NOT AS EASY AS IT LOOKS

Value intelligence can be a huge asset for B2B marketers, fueling their campaigns with business value content and messaging that appeals to a range of potential customers seeking meaningful business outcomes. But to create those value-based assets, marketers need help from different functional groups across the enterprise. That's not always an easy job.

A case in point is one of the world's most respected global SaaS companies, which wanted to glean value intelligence insights from several groups. These included the value engineering/value management program, which usually supports the sales organization by generating value forecasts and business cases *before* the sale. It also wanted to pick the brains of its customer success program, which routinely delivers "value realization" assessments that quantify the various business benefits the customer sees *after* the sale.

By bringing the two groups together and sharing their customer insights, the company's marketing organization hoped it could create unique customer stories with compelling proof points that demonstrated the business value realized by customers. The initiative was expected to be easy; all the

---

[5] "Intricately's 2021 Cloud Marketing Maturity Model," Mainstay, 2021.

marketing team needed was to pull in business value assessments from both teams along with some strong before-after use cases.

But it wasn't as easy as the marketers had hoped, as they faced both organizational and technical challenges:

- Marketing content designers and writers got bogged down translating detailed Microsoft PowerPoint documents into simple stories.
- The sales value management team and the customer success team lacked the bandwidth to support these writers due to customer time commitments.
- Much of the information was confidential, and the writers couldn't easily normalize and blind the data.
- Each team used similar but different terminology for business benefits and outcomes.

This SaaS company's experience underscores the fact that just having a leading value engineering and customer success program does not automatically translate into value intelligence that marketers can easily use. We believe several common organizational hurdles stand in the way of success for B2B marketers:

- First, product marketing tends to play second fiddle to sales. That's because CEOs often come from stints in sales organizations, which are often viewed as being on the "front lines" with the customer and a clear revenue generator. Marketing departments, by contrast, often struggle to demonstrate substantial ROI for their programs.
- Second, marketing can suffer from cyclical budget ups and downs. During strong economic cycles, for example, marketing is often asked to do more with limited team resources as more spending flows to advertising and other large marketing programs. And during weak economic cycles, marketing is often the first group to be cut and takes the biggest resource hit during a layoff. It seems like every three or four years, shifts in the economic cycle ripple through marketing organizations, creating staff disruptions and discontinuities in messaging and events, making it difficult to show consistent ROI results.
- Third, product marketing and sales teams often don't see eye-to-eye when it comes to go-to-market strategies. Reasons can vary from personality differences between executives, to turf battles, and to disagreements among stakeholders about where to deploy limited capital.

These product marketing barriers are particularly important when implementing an account-based marketing program. ABM relies on a strong, integrated partnership between sales and marketing. It requires agile content development that is customized to fit specific customer needs and opportunities, and a leadership team that looks at marketing and sales as an integrated function, not as separate and unequal departments.

Because of these dynamics, product marketing can easily develop some bad habits, including:

- Teams that are reluctant to work closely with sales
- Stubbornly high operating expenses
- Go-to-market campaigns can take months to build awareness and generate sales
- Marketing assets that are out of touch with customer conversations and needs

To execute successful ABM strategies, marketers will need to improve their current set of skills, tools, and organizational processes, empowering them to zero in on specific customer groups. Marketers will not only need to identify the top customer segments for their products, but also understand the nuances and unique attributes of the customers within each segment. They will also need to identify new digital tools to gather customer data and build comprehensive customer profiles that are both accurate and relevant.

Armed with new-and-improved customer insights, ABM-based marketing and sales teams can design effective product marketing programs that deliver useful value intelligence tailored for each customer. That means targeting the right buyer groups and their individual motivations for making investment decisions. What's more, much of the same customer insights that product marketers create for their sales teams can also be used upstream by revenue marketers looking to better target prospects through their digital marketing programs, trade shows, corporate events, and other market awareness activities.

Revenue Marketing: Large Nets and High Costs

In the last decade, the B2B buying process has changed dramatically, with many customers now preferring digital channels over person-to-person interactions. Gartner, for example, says that 75 percent of B2B buyers prefer a rep-free sales experience.[6] And our experiences working with

---

[6] "B2B Buying: How Top CSOs and CMOs Optimize the Journey," Gartner (https://www.gartner.com/en/sales/insights/b2b-buying-journey).

CIOs and enterprise technology buyers over the past decades support this view. Increasingly, we've seen that most buyers, especially early in the decision-making process, want to do their own research to understand the competitive landscape. As part of this effort, they may leverage research from leading industry analysts, such as Forrester Research or Gartner, to get an objective view of the market landscape. They'll also review content posted on vendor websites, including whitepapers and case studies, and learn more about solutions by attending webinars, conferences, and industry trade shows.

As more customers embrace self-service product research, a greater burden is placed on vendors to make sure their company is presenting the right content, to the right buyer, at the right time. To do this, the company's product marketing team needs to work closely with its *revenue marketing* team, which is responsible for drawing in potential new customers (leads) with compelling content and messaging. But revenue marketers face several challenges as they attempt to create a successful digital marketing program.

REVENUE MARKETERS: A KEY DRIVER OF GROWTH

In their quest for new customers, most B2B companies rely on a team of digital marketers tasked with driving revenue growth through targeted digital marketing strategies. The team often works with advertising agencies to develop digital campaigns to build awareness and generate leads. Revenue marketing is all about populating the very top of the *sales funnel*. And as you'll see, it's an area where the combination of value marketing and AI can make a big difference.

Digital Marketing Challenges

Capturing leads can be expensive. B2B marketers spend millions on digital advertising campaigns that require months, if not years, to pay dividends. During that time, executives have to exercise extreme patience as their marketers methodically design and ramp up campaigns and steadily build an audience. Unfortunately, these programs are almost always the first to be cut during an economic downturn, the plug being pulled just when product awareness is spreading.

Thus, setting aside sufficient budget can be a major challenge for digital marketing campaigns, which can include acquiring and sustaining annual prospect target lists and paying for advertising and social media programs. Expenses can run from the low six digits for an "entry-level" program to millions for large enterprises. But despite the hefty outlays, the resulting hit rates and qualified leads can be surprisingly meager.

The other challenge for revenue marketers is content creation. Catchy phrases or splashy graphics are not enough to turn awareness into interest. To succeed, campaigns must speak to the heart of what drives business value for their potential customer. Once again, value management can play an important role.

Realize that nearly everybody you reach out to at the top of the funnel will be *digital cold calls*. Like it or not, many of your prospects will feel bombarded by things they didn't ask for, whether it's spam emails, out-of-the-blue LinkedIn invites, or off-topic Google Ads. The challenge for revenue marketers is to break through this digital clutter by combining spot-on content with marketing automation systems that can harvest only the most promising leads for their inside sales teams to act on.

VM PRO TIP

To help drive a successful demand-gen campaign, consider tapping an external ecosystem of marketing partners, including data scientists, program coordinators, and digital channel and advertising experts.

STUMBLING BLOCKS FOR REVENUE MARKETERS

- Failing to fully leverage both outside data providers and internal customer data to create ideal customer profiles (ICPs).

- Throwing too wide of a net for potential leads, leading to high vendor costs for list purchases and digital ad campaigns.

- Dropped handoffs when moving prospects from marketing qualified leads (MQLs) to sales qualified leads (SQLs), slowing deal velocity.

Event Marketing Challenges

During the pandemic, large corporate events and industry trade shows[7] were largely put on hold. In its place, companies scrambled to put on

---

[7] Some of the more popular B2B tradeshows we attend include AWS re:Invent, Salesforce Dreamforce, Oracle CloudWorld, Retail's Big Show, and the RSA Conference.

virtual events with mixed results. We think these large virtual events are now behind us, with companies eagerly embracing the return of in-person events—and for good reason: People crave human-to-human interaction. The legacy of the pandemic lives on, however, with many companies promoting hybrid events that include a "virtual add-on" to the in-person event. These have been successful in extending the reach of these conferences by giving people who can't make the trip in person a convenient way to participate.

Still, hosting large corporate events and trade shows that bring in tens of thousands of their customers and prospects for a weeklong event remains a challenge. We see this in our work with marketing teams at many large B2B technology companies. These challenges include:

- **High costs of renting floor space and hosting booths:** Entry points can be in the six figures and up to seven figures for the top sponsors of these events.

- **Attracting prospects and creating worthwhile leads:** It's often hard to avoid booth experiences that aren't dominated by tchotchke giveaways but instead foster meaningful conversations that lead to high-potential prospects.

- **Ensuring event content that demonstrates industry leadership:** This means building strong brand differentiation by providing value intelligence-based messaging.

Unfortunately, too many enterprise B2B tech companies treat annual trade shows and conferences as a necessary evil with the goal of simply showing industry leadership and maintaining market momentum. Financially, companies just want to break even financially on the event. Our view of these in-person gatherings is more strategic—they in fact provide a motherload of opportunities for revenue marketers to deepen and expand the ABM programs they've developed for each of the attendees. The key challenge will be integrating personalized event activities with ABM-level insights to accelerate the buyer journey. (See the section "What's Next: Value Management Marketing Powered by AI," to find out how AI can help.)

Corporate Marketing: Siloed Function, Limited ROI Visibility

Corporate marketing is a valuable part of any large B2B enterprise—and its sizable budgets reflect that fact. Encompassing advertising, PR, events, sports team sponsorships, and more, corporate marketing strives to build the brand equity of the company, positioning the company as an industry leader and growing margins in the process. From a value management point of view, corporate marketing events must communicate meaningful strategic and financial value to its customers and new sales channels in order to generate significant revenue upside potential.

We recently had the opportunity to do just that when we were asked by a global technology company to assess the potential return on investment of becoming a major sponsor of an upcoming Olympics. It was fascinating to see how the company's executive team and board of directors viewed this opportunity from both a brand equity and ROI perspective. The initiative would not only help the company showcase their products but also how they could drive business value for customers and bring in new sales in the process.

Given the massive spending that sponsoring the world's most recognized sporting event would require, we were skeptical at first that we could justify the client's investment. However, academic research and our subsequent financial analysis suggested otherwise. It pointed to the likelihood that the Olympic sponsorship would in fact generate a significant sales lift, more than offsetting the cost of the initiative.

As we developed our recommendations, we recognized that securing a positive ROI was heavily dependent on executing a well-thought-out sales game plan. The effort would involve organizing massive financial and human resources, creating and communicating unique Olympics-related solutions for their customers—generating incremental sales to drive the ROI of sponsorship. Given the size of the investment, the marketing group was required to monitor results over a five-year-plus period and report back to the board of directors and CEO on the performance of the sponsorship initiative. The effort is the poster child for an ABM-led effort, with a new level of engagement between marketing and sales teams as they worked together to integrate sales tools with marketing content creation and forge closer ties with customers and executives over the five-year-plus period.

Working side by side with our client to plan for the Olympics gave us a deeper appreciation of marketing's role in engaging a diverse ecosystem of both internal and external players to build an ABM strategy for this event, including company sales teams and outside marketing partners and vendors. We saw that only by collaborating with these broader ecosystem partners could the marketing team deliver the exceptional business outcomes we witnessed. But another lesson dawned on us— namely that the marketing initiative could have been a greater success if the messaging was more value focused and featured more industry- and customer-specific ROI insights.

The management consulting firm McKinsey would not have been surprised by this experience. It recently found that top-performing marketers were more likely than their peers to be part of a "networked organization" and met more frequently with other parts of the business to create and deliver *customer experience journeys*.[8] As shown in Figure 4.2, B2B marketing leaders can move to a more collaborative and agile organizational model when it's supported by a diverse partner ecosystem, enabling companies to align more quickly to the dynamics of modern customer demand.

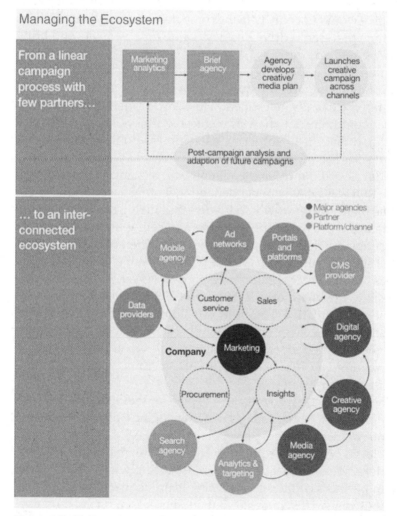

Figure 4.2: McKinsey's view of managing marketing partnerships (internal and external)

---

[8] "Building a marketing organization that drives growth today," McKinsey & Co., August 2017.

The Current State of Value Management in Marketing

What is the current state of marketing from a value management perspective? Frankly, we're seeing a practice that is just starting out and showing ample room for improvement. But there is a gathering momentum in the field, with pockets of good content and the emergence of first-mover industries that are adopting innovative ABM digital practices. We are also seeing the growth of new technologies that can potentially lay the groundwork for AI-driven value management in B2B marketing. Among the current leaders in value management in marketing is Hewlett Packard Enterprises (HPE), whose wireless networking division, HPE Aruba Networking, has leveraged its value engineering team in the sales organization to boost its marketing performance.

Framing the value conversation with potential customers early in their buying life cycle is one of the keys to marketing success, says Paul Randlesome, Value Management Leader at HPE Aruba Networking. "Many of our prospective customers are doing self-service research on our website," he says. "We need to be thoughtful in our value content as to not set expectations with overly inflated benefits."

That means sticking to realistic estimates of potential value. Randlesome adds that "Our best practice is to provide value intelligence thought leadership by providing business impact KPI ranges and percentages to communicate customer business outcomes that we can defend." His team plays an important role in defining value messaging across HPE's buyer journey, from marketing to sales to customer success. Randlesome adds: "Our ability to provide quantifiable business benefits is one of the advantages that my team can provide to support our customer go-to-market activities."

Randlesome's team of industry experts also packages HPE's value intelligence into individual business use cases. "We want to demonstrate to our prospective customers that we understand their specific business pain points and ensure that the customer understands how we can solve for their unique challenges," he says.

We're seeing more companies today starting to mimic HPE's value-based marketing approach by scaling their existing value engineering programs. There's still a large gap to be closed, however, before most are capable of achieving a mature AI-VM marketing function.

Here's a brief summary of the value-management capabilities, coverage, and customer outcomes among leading B2B marketing teams:

Capabilities   While there are a number of marketing organizations that exhibit strong value management capabilities, most are still immature. To grow their capabilities, marketing teams will need to add new value management marketing skills to develop compelling business impact use cases, value drivers, partner solution ecosystems, and GenAI learning model development. Processes will need to be streamlined and automated to help scale value management programs, mobilizing marketing technologies and data systems to nurture future AI platforms. New AI-VM marketing programs will likely tap into additional data sources to provide automated assistants that can scale existing marketing resources. Organizationally, marketing will need to become a more networked organization, as McKinsey recommends, and tear down siloes between lines of business. Funding also needs to be better defended, reducing budget volatility to allow marketing programs and events to capture their full potential.

Coverage   We are seeing more companies implementing or piloting value management capabilities in selected industries and for specific solutions. For many B2B companies, marketing teams can be stretched thin across solutions and industries, making the quality and effectiveness of the content difficult to maintain. Top-of-funnel programs typically cast a wide net because detailed ideal customer profiles (ICPs) are difficult to develop and match to prospects. Top-of-funnel lead scoring and handling can be complicated by organizational barriers and limited engagement telemetry. Geographic regional support as well as channel support can also fall short because of limited resources.

Customer Outcomes   In general, marketing teams do a poor job of identifying and monitoring customer outcomes and KPIs, so they often struggle to prove the ROI of their activities. For example, proving that "downstream" sales were the result of "upstream" marketing messaging and prospect engagement activities is often discounted by the company's leadership team. More often than not, a successful deal will be credited to sales activities closer to the time of the sale. Improving win rates based on upstream product positioning, value proposition messaging, and industry use cases can be hampered by a lack of resources, limited value intelligence content, and gaps in segment or solution coverage. Meanwhile, reducing customer churn can be limited by a disconnect with customer success teams, and improving customer profitability can be difficult because poor coordination between sales, value management, and customer success team means that upsell and cross-sell opportunities are often missed.

As we look beyond the maturity level of most B2B marketing organizations today, we can see how the adoption of customer value management powered by AI could provide the wherewithal—namely the skills, processes, and technologies—that B2B enterprises will need to modernize their marketing operations and compete in the next digital economy.

As we'll discuss in the next section, AI-driven value management offers the unique ability to bridge the gap across marketing, sales, and emerging ecosystem partners. Marketers can now target the right prospects with the right value proposition, save costs by pinpointing prospects with the most revenue potential, and link upstream funnel activity to downstream outcomes. For the first time, organizations will be able to prove the ROI of their marketing programs and smartly manage the constantly shifting budgets and resources that marketing teams have faced for decades.

What's Next: Value Management Marketing Powered by AI

In our view, adopting AI-powered value management for marketing will be a natural evolution for most B2B marketing organizations, building on the enterprise technology investments they've already made. Significant investments in marketing modernization have helped companies take small steps toward ABM strategies by automating digital campaign management. These include investments in automation tools such as HubSpot, Marketo, and Eloqua; value automation via platforms such as Mainstay's Advisor Platform; and sales enablement automation using CRM solutions such as Salesforce. All of these investments provide a solid foundation for creating a new AI-driven value management marketing capability, which we will outline in this chapter.

Infusing marketing programs with AI-driven value management processes and technologies is certain to drive yet another massive transformation to B2B marketing, requiring teams to rethink many of the core aspects of their go-to-market strategies and ABM programs.

We will likely see further advancement of their data management capabilities and a significant retooling of their organizational models to deliver 2-to-the-power-of-3 revenue results.

Let's now lay out the blueprint for the AI-VM marketing organization using new value management methods supercharged by AI technology. We'll look at each part of the functions laid out earlier in the chapter: product marketing, revenue marketing, and corporate marketing.

The New Product Marketer: Enhancing Solution Positioning with Value Intelligence

How will product marketing teams work in the future, powered by AI-driven value management? We believe the methods and technologies laid out in this book will transform the everyday lives of product marketers, helping optimize product positioning, pricing, promotions, and customer reference programs. Informed by AI-generated product performance insights, marketers will gain a crystal-clear understanding of the ROI of all their future programs.

As we described earlier, attempts to scale ABM strategies have been a challenge for most B2B companies. Let's break down the key challenges and how AI-VM marketing will be a game changer on removing critical barriers to success.

By value intelligence, we mean the ability to articulate the business impact of a company's products and services and in the process show a clear and positive ROI for the buyer. For product marketers, acquiring customer insights to develop this messaging can be challenging. Customer insights can be housed across a myriad of systems and can even reside with channel partners. The data can be spread across applications, spreadsheets, and handwritten notes. All these data complexities and aggregation challenges make the data difficult to harvest and analyze.

That's all about to change. AI-driven value management can become a new resource for marketers to create value intelligence content quickly and accurately. The emerging adoption of AI-VM will transform the way prospects are targeted; how marketing content is used to build digital relationships with prospects; and how marketers will continually improve their market positioning, pricing, and placement of products going forward.

Let's discuss how AI can play a crucial role in achieving value intelligence at scale across the four phases of the product marketing life cycle (see Figure 4.3).

Figure 4.3: The four phases of product marketing

Market Positioning with Value Intelligence Powered by AI   Positioning your product in the market is crucial to business success. Often the process involves creating a *value tree* with associated *value drivers*. This forms the basis of a value intelligence framework—a set of value drivers and associated value benchmarks—that lies at the heart of the product's market positioning. However, compiling the data to build an effective market position can be tedious and time consuming. A well-trained generative AI assistant can help streamline the process by quickly finding and analyzing data across the enterprise—and from external sources—to develop your market positioning at a fraction of the cost.

> At the heart of value intelligence is a management consulting framework called a "value tree" (see Figure 4.4). A value tree provides a structured breakdown of "value categories," such as revenue and cost savings, into "value drivers," such as cost per MIP, labor costs, power savings; benchmarks (such as percentage and dollar savings), and related assumptions.

Optimize Pricing with AI-Powered Value Intelligence   Similarly, pricing can benefit from better understanding a product's business impact. Instead of setting prices based on traditional market elements such as the competitive pricing landscape, companies can develop AI-VM pricing models based on the quantified business benefits achieved by adopting these solutions. For example, if a customer service SaaS solution can drive a 2X productivity result for a contact center customer, then the SaaS provider can look to capture a good portion of that cost savings in their pricing models. This approach provides the contact center customer with an adequate ROI that meets their investment hurdle rates, while the SaaS margins are maximized by capturing the remaining cost savings impact above and beyond their customer's hurdle rate.

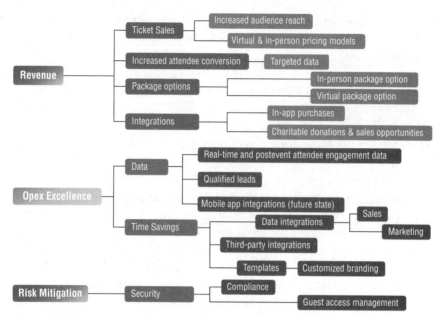

Figure 4.4: Example of a value tree from a past client's product positioning

Marketing and Promotion with AI Value Intelligence   Marketing and promotion will benefit from AI value intelligence in a couple of key areas. First, as McKinsey discussed in its vision of the future of marketing, effective collaboration across a number of external and internal marketing partners will be essential to the success of marketing and promotion programs.

Generative AI will play a collaborative role in achieving this goal. For example, an AI marketing assistant will be able to take the value intelligence content developed in the market positioning phase and automatically generate a portfolio of go-to-market assets that support a diverse set of promotional campaigns, such as social media tiles, ROI whitepapers, thought leadership blogs, customer success stories, and more. Marketers will still need to review, refine, and finalize these assets, but their AI marketing assistant can significantly streamline that effort and ensure they are communicated and shared across the partners, speeding execution of the programs.

Customer Reference with AI Value Intelligence   Finally, the ability to scale customer references can be achieved through virtual reference assistants. The assistants will be able to comb through sales and customer service presentations and review solution usage data to identify the right customer reference targets. Once approved by the references team, the reference assistant can even conduct a virtual interview with the customer and combine these results with existing customer value intelligence data to draft a customer reference story. Also, the reference assistant can recommend customers to be added to the company's customer advisory board, based on value intelligence criteria such as customer's influence value, level of maturity with your products, and the customer's willingness to promote the company as a trusted partner.

We've summarized the GenAI marketing approach and its benefits in Figure 4.5 and associated GenAI use cases in Table 4.1.

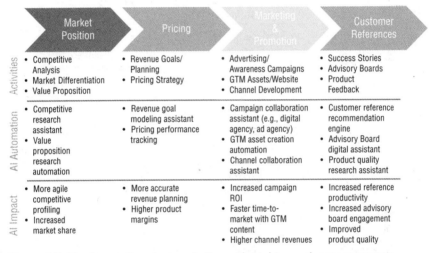

	Market Position	Pricing	Marketing & Promotion	Customer References
Activities	• Competitive Analysis • Market Differentiation • Value Proposition	• Revenue Goals/ Planning • Pricing Strategy	• Advertising/ Awareness Campaigns • GTM Assets/Website • Channel Development	• Success Stories • Advisory Boards • Product Feedback
AI Automation	• Competitive research assistant • Value proposition research automation	• Revenue goal modeling assistant • Pricing performance tracking	• Campaign collaboration assistant (e.g., digital agency, ad agency) • GTM asset creation automation • Channel collaboration assistant	• Customer reference recommendation engine • Advisory Board digital assistant • Product quality research assistant
AI Impact	• More agile competitive profiling • Increased market share	• More accurate revenue planning • Higher product margins	• Increased campaign ROI • Faster time-to-market with GTM content • Higher channel revenues	• Increased reference productivity • Increased advisory board engagement • Improved product quality

Figure 4.5: The future of product marketing with AI-driven value management

VM PRO TIP

Start using generative AI tools to draft value intelligence marketing content on the fly, allowing you to reduce manual efforts and enhance the quantification of value across your go-to-market assets. This will help to cost-effectively scale value intelligence marketing activities across the enterprise and for your partner community.

Table 4.1:   GenAI product marketing assistant use cases

#	ACTIVITY	SOURCE	AI-ASSISTED ACTIONS
1	Market Positioning Research	Product systems, value engineering systems, customer success systems, third-party industry research sources	Auto-generate drafts of a solution's value tree and competitive positioning analyses to streamline product marketing's ability to build a value intelligence-based value proposition.
2	Pricing Assistant	Product systems, third-party research systems, value engineering systems, customer success systems	Auto-generate reports based on value intelligence/customer impact and competitive pricing insights to maximize margin and share of market.
3	Marketing & Promotion Assistant	Internal CRM, value engineering systems, customer success systems, partner CRM	Assist in collaboration across go-to-market teams and partners by generating multiple formats of value intelligence content to meet the needs across all channels and customer journey stages.
4	Customer Reference Assistant	Internal CRM, value engineering systems, customer success systems, partner CRM	Assist in generation of value intelligence-based customer reference stories.

The New Revenue Marketer: Automating and Scaling ABM with Value Intelligence

Revenue marketers are given a simple but critical assignment: generate leads for sales teams that will be converted into revenue. But that can be hard when marketers are working in a vacuum, unaware of the knowledge and insights that sales teams—and other organizations such as customer success teams—gather every day. We believe it's essential that revenue marketing teams start their AI-VM transformation by building a closer partnership with sales. Indeed, our research found that if marketing and sales teams work together to implement innovative ABM strategies, they can increase top-line performance measurably (see Figure 4.6).

The positive impacts we found in our research were huge, including 76 percent higher ROI, 55 percent greater revenues, and so on.[9]

76% HIGHER ROI[5]	By aligning and focusing sales and marketing resources on a smaller but higher potential set of prospective costumers.
55% HIGHER REVENUES[5]	By targeting the right organizations with assets that better connect your solutions with their challenges.
16% HIGHER DEAL SIZES[6]	By focusing on targets that have business needs that require your solutions.
13% INCREASED SALES VELOCITY[6]	By leveraging more direct marketing to start with a more targeted view of how your solutions benefit the prospect.
34% IMPROVED REPUTATION[5]	By using data to gain insights on your targets and creating marketing plans that directly speak to those targets.
16% INCREASED PIPELINE[6]	By harnessing deeper insights based on data-driven targeting to identify additional market opportunities.

Figure 4.6: Future state ABM KPIs

As we described in the previous section, the average B2B revenue marketer may find it challenging to shift to tighter integration with sales and value engineering teams. By successfully adopting an ABM program, however, marketers will naturally bring these functions together and put the company in a position to generate 2X or greater marketing qualified leads (MQLs).

We think ABM will become an important part of future revenue marketing strategies. One of our clients, Intricately, recently acquired by HG Insights, gave us a preview of where we believe future revenue marketing is heading. Instead of starting with a "broad net" of potential leads, a next-gen revenue strategy based on an intelligent ABM approach will "flip the script" by zeroing in on a highly targeted set of accounts

---

[9] "Intricately's 2021 Cloud Marketing Maturity Model," Mainstay, 2021.

with a high probability of revenue success. The funnel expands from there as multiple buying decision-makers are identified and targeted within each account (see Figure 4.7).

The Next-Gen Account-Based Revenue Strategy

TRADITIONAL REVENUE APPROACH	NEXT-GEN ACCOUNT-BASED REVENUE APPROACH
Wide Net Approach	Deeper Insights on Smaller Set of Prospects
Expensive & Arbitrary Lead Lists	Marketing/Sales/Sales Operations Coordinated GTM
Limited Marketing and Sales Strategy Alignment	Limited Marketing and Sales Strategy Alignment
Quantity over Quality	GTM Resources Focused to Top Prospects

VS

Figure 4.7: Next-generation account-based revenue strategy

HG Insights' success in generating leads (and ultimately increasing revenue) in the cloud-infrastructure industry shows that ABM could be just the tip of the iceberg for B2B marketers. As products and services continue to digitize, access to high-quality data to target new leads will become the norm for B2B companies.

As you'll see in a moment, ABM programs can be enhanced significantly with the addition of value intelligence and AI solutions, helping reduce friction across teams and ultimately closing the gap between marketing and sales. ABM-based demand-gen programs can now grow quickly with minimal investment, generating impressive returns.

Let's look closely at how a combination of value intelligence and AI solutions can help revenue marketers execute a more efficient and productive digital demand-gen campaign. The campaign has four key steps:

1. List definition
2. Content development
3. Campaign design
4. Lead management

Value intelligence supported by AI solutions will improve each of these steps (see Figure 4.8).

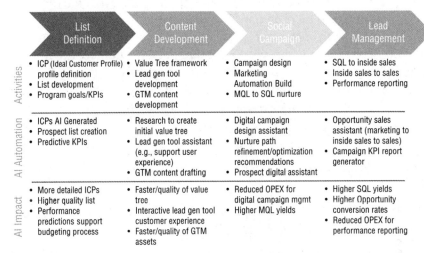

	List Definition	Content Development	Social Campaign	Lead Management
Activities	• ICP (Ideal Customer Profile) profile definition • List development • Program goals/KPIs	• Value Tree framework • Lead gen tool development • GTM content development	• Campaign design • Marketing Automation Build • MQL to SQL nurture	• SQL to inside sales • Inside sales to sales • Performance reporting
AI Automation	• ICPs AI Generated • Prospect list creation • Predictive KPIs	• Research to create initial value tree • Lead gen tool assistant (e.g., support user experience) • GTM content drafting	• Digital campaign design assistant • Nurture path refinement/optimization recommendations • Prospect digital assistant	• Opportunity sales assistant (marketing to inside sales to sales) • Campaign KPI report generator
AI Impact	• More detailed ICPs • Higher quality list • Performance predictions support budgeting process	• Faster/quality of value tree • Interactive lead gen tool customer experience • Faster/quality of GTM assets	• Reduced OPEX for digital campaign mgmt • Higher MQL yields	• Higher SQL yields • Higher Opportunity conversion rates • Reduced OPEX for performance reporting

Figure 4.8: Demand-gen programs powered by AI

As shown in Figure 4.8, AI solutions can help manage each part of a demand-gen program. As more marketers begin using new AI-driven demand-gen assistants, they will discover a host of advantages, including the ability to create higher-quality targeting lists, build better lead-gen communications and tools, more easily nurture leads, and manage the transition from MQLs to sales qualified leads (SQLs) and beyond. What's more, AI applications can help revenue marketers stretch their budgets by reducing the cost of buying prospect lists, creating content, running marketing campaigns, and managing leads and opportunities. Let's start with how AI can reinvent the way revenue marketers target prospects.

Improving Digital Demand-Gen "Targeting" Using Value Intelligence

Simply put, AI-led value intelligence will enable revenue marketers to "flip the funnel." Here's how it would work. First, AI solutions can make it faster and easier to create an ICP (Ideal Customer Profile), a key part of demand-gen targeting. AI revenue assistants will help by rapidly ingesting the value intelligence market positioning provided by product marketing.

The assistant will summarize key aspects of a solution's value proposition and integrate relevant buyer personas, industries, and market and geographical attributes to create truly ideal customer profiles. These profiles can then be matched against a set of targeted prospect profiles to generate a concise list of high-potential targets. The AI assistant can then match these target profiles to the right messaging that the revenue marketer can use in their demand-gen campaign.

In our work with clients, we're already seeing seeds of this approach take root. For example, our work with HG Insights demonstrated that a data-centric, value-led ABM program can deliver significantly greater returns compared to a traditional demand-gen approach. There were three main advantages to creating more detailed target profiles:

- Clients could "flip the funnel"—generating greater conversion rates and reducing costs.

- It validated and enhanced the value intelligence approach to marketing.

- It supported the ABM-approach by providing recommendations on the best journeys for customers.

Although at the time of our study our client was not using AI modeling, the detailed data analytics used by its platform broke new ground in demand-gen programs. In fact, the analytics-based ABM approach to demand management pioneered by Intricately represents the future of how B2B companies will drive top-of-funnel demand using AI-driven value management.

Revenue marketing assistants powered by generative AI will be instrumental in scaling this approach at B2B enterprises. Indeed, much of the manual effort needed to generate ideal customer profiles and develop value intelligence can be automated using generative AI tools.

We have identified three use cases using AI-based solutions to target prospects in the context of a modern ABM program:

- The demand-gen AI assistant analyzes thousands of customer attributes to develop a detailed set of ICPs (Ideal Customer Profiles).

- The assistant compares the ICPs against prospect attributes to develop a list of the best target accounts.

- The assistant provides the revenue marketing team with recommendations on how to engage these targets to maximize conversion rates.

Table 4.2 lays out these three use cases.

Table 4.2:   GenAI demand-generation assistant targeting use cases

#	ACTIVITY	SOURCE	AI-ASSISTED ACTIONS
1	Ideal Customer Profile (ICP) Mining	Web, internal CRM, social media	Auto-generate ICP list based on company CRM system, event data, social media interactions. ICP can be refined over time as results from the sales funnel are fed back into the model to increase targeting accuracy.
2	Solution Impact Digital Research	Internal product systems, third-party research systems	Automatically mine target's solution usage data to assess maturity, or other aspects that can predict value opportunities. AI demand-gen assistant provides value intelligence positioning recommendations.
3	ABM Strategies	Internal CRM, value management systems	Provide recommendations on marketing and sales tactics such as prospect nurturing paths, inside sales messaging, account team tactics.

Using Value Intelligence to Create a Demand-Gen "Hook"

The "hook" is probably the most important part of a demand-gen campaign. The hook is a collection of marketing assets—something as simple as a digital ad, video, or blog—that catches the eye of potential customers and motivates them to take the next step toward a sales engagement. The action could be something as simple as inputting their contact information into an online form.

The AI assistant can help marketers create the hook by identifying the product's go-to-market positioning and finding the right value intelligence-based content out of a mountain of assets created by the product marketing or value management teams. The assistant can then position the content in the appropriate formats as part of a specific digital demand generation campaign.

CREATING A DIGITAL "HOOK"

The success of digital marketing campaigns hinges on delivering content and tools that entice a prospect to pony up their contact information. The prospect knows that by providing their information they will be targeted by the vendor, so they are often very careful when making that decision. The asset that convinces prospects to share their information we call the "hook." Typical assets that can be positioned as a hook include ROI whitepapers, webinar recordings, paid-for analyst studies, solution maturity tools, benefit calculators, and industry benchmark reports.

Revenue marketers can maximize conversion rates by offering relevant value intelligence content that supports the buyer's research process. For example, an HR manager researching talent management solutions may not readily share their contact information after reading a simple customer story that lacks credible proof of business value. But that same manager may sign up for more information if it is a research whitepaper that presents quantified KPIs and descriptions of how and why these benefits were achieved.

This is where an AI assistant can help by simplifying the experience for the HR manager who is researching your solution, for example, by providing conversational answers to the manager's questions:

- HR manager: "How does your solution accelerate the hiring process?"

- AI solution assistant: "Our solution has reduced time to hire metrics such as time to offer, time to accept and time to onboard by 50 percent over conventional processes. Would you like to learn more?"

For the demand-gen teams, the AI assistant can help marketers reduce the effort it takes to build value intelligence content. Two simple use cases include:

- Identifying and quantifying value intelligence benchmarks for lead-gen tools

- Generating value intelligence reports, such as industry whitepapers

Table 4.3 details the AI-assisted actions for each of these use cases.

Table 4.3: Revenue marketing assistant hook use cases

#	ACTIVITY	SOURCE	AI-ASSISTED ACTIONS
1	Customer Solution Assistant	Internal product systems	Provide conversational solution research support to prospects looking at your solution but have not engaged your company yet (top of funnel).

#	ACTIVITY	SOURCE	AI-ASSISTED ACTIONS
2	Value Intelligence Tool Assistant	Internal product systems, value engineering systems	Provide the value engineer and revenue marketing teams with customer value intelligence insights (e.g., customer performance KPIs) to create compelling lead-gen tools.
3	Value Intelligence Reports	Internal CRM, value engineering systems	Automatically generate drafts of value-based whitepapers (e.g., industry ROI whitepapers) based on content available in reference stories, product marketing research, partner/third-party research.

VM PRO TIP

Product marketers serve as a leading voice in account-based marketing programs. Along with other ABM team members from sales and customer success programs, they can form a "think tank" to develop an effective go-to-market value proposition.

READY FOR 2X MORE LEADS?

Our research shows that revenue marketers that host value intelligence-based tools, such as benefit calculators, solution assessment tools, can expect to capture nearly 2X more leads. In fact, our customer data shows an average 12–15 percent conversion rate compared to the industry average of about 7 percent.

VM PRO TIP

Marketing data partners will be essential to the future success of your business. Start by identifying partners that can bring unique and complementary data sources, then jointly pilot marketing programs that test the effectiveness of different market hypotheses.

Boosting the ROI of Corporate Events and Trade Shows

By deploying new AI solutions and value management strategies, revenue marketers now have a great opportunity to reinvent corporate events and trade shows and realize greater ROI from these key marketing investments. Unlocking new revenue opportunities will hinge on marketers finding new ways to transform the event experience, including:

- Upgrading value intelligence content and messaging for eventgoers
- Providing individualized/personalized experiences for participants
- Offering engaging interactive booth experiences

Leveraging AI-Driven Value Intelligence Content

One of the simplest and most effective ways to improve revenue potential—and overall success—of company events and trade shows is to up level the content you present to participants. Armed with value intelligence messaging, executives and marketing teams can now speak directly to the business-value issues that are top of mind for decision-makers in the audience—your potential customers. Too often, we've attended events where the "show" is better than the "message," meaning they were devoid of much-needed business value content. Thus, a prime opportunity to communicate your company's thought leadership and unique capabilities is wasted. That can change by leveraging a value intelligence engine (see the "New Product Marketer" section) to deliver the business-value insights that the vast majority of potential customers are looking for at these events.

Once again, AI tools can be a powerful tool for helping marketing teams prepare and orchestrate corporate events quickly and accurately. Table 4.4 describes just a few key use cases that can be assisted with AI-powered apps and tools that are integrated with existing business systems.

Table 4.4: Value intelligence AI event use cases

#	ACTIVITY	DATA SOURCE	AI-ASSISTED ACTIONS
1	Keynote/ Session Content Assistant	Internal product systems	Provide conversational solution research support to executives and marketing teams looking to collect industry trends, industry value propositions, customer KPI/success stories.
2	Value Intelligence Assistants	Internal product systems, value engineering systems	Provide event staff with an AI assistant to address any value intelligence questions they may have to support customer conversations.

Individualized Participant Experiences

We've all experienced the feeling of being distracted and lost at gigantic trade shows and corporate events. Your potential customers feel the same way, as they struggle to choose which sessions are worthwhile to attend and who they should meet and when. What they need is an event agenda tailored to their specific business needs and interests. Today, that effort is typically a self-service function. When participants register for the event, there are "tracks" to help them select and organize their sessions and activities. The best-case scenario for participants is when the vendor's account manager helps set the schedule and suggests selective executive-only sessions or social networking activities.

There's a better way to engage with current and potential customers at trade shows and corporate events. It's called an AI digital concierge and it promises to be a game changer for participants. The AI-enabled concierge helps set the participant's agenda well before attending the event and schedules time with the sponsor's on-site experts and executives. The digital concierge checks in with the participants during the event to help adjust the agenda in real time based on their experiences at the event (see Table 4.5). Informed by ABM insights collected over the lifespan of interactions with that customer (or similar company profiles), the AI-VM powered concierge will be a game changer for marketers staging corporate events and trade shows in the near future.

Table 4.5:   Individualized participant experiences AI use cases

#	ACTIVITY	DATA SOURCE	AI-ASSISTED ACTIONS
1	Participant AI Digital Concierge	Internal product systems, value engineering systems, CRM systems, customer success systems	AI-driven assistants provide event participants (customers/prospects) with recommendations on sessions to attend, booth activities relevant to their needs, social networking activities, and company experts and executives that are available to support specific needs they may have.

Continues

Table 4.5 (*continued*)

#	ACTIVITY	DATA SOURCE	AI-ASSISTED ACTIONS
2	Participant AI Value Digital Consultant	Internal product systems, value engineering systems, CRM systems, customer success systems	The AI value consultants can consult participants on specific value-related questions that may present itself during the conference. The digital consultant can use participant profile information (customer insights, industry and company profiles, conversationally gained content) to recommend solutions that address the customers'/prospects' specific business needs or strategic objectives and even recommend specific research sources to enhance the participants' knowledge.

Interactive Booth Experiences

One of the biggest areas for improvement at trade shows and corporate events is the booth experience. We've seen some impressive ones over the years and digital media has made them even more engaging, with innovative demos and prototypes that demonstrate industry leadership. The best booth experiences need to be forward-looking, and the staff must be knowledgeable and experienced—capable of answering questions related not only to the product's feature and functions, but how the company's solutions may integrate into the prospect's specific business challenges or technology architectures.

AI can provide a new way to deliver on this objective. The combination of value intelligence content that is being developed by the product marketing team, with the ABM content collected across all go-to-market teams, can turn the one-on-one booth experience into highly productive value-based conversation. This will transform the nature of the booth experience and accelerate the buyer journey (see Table 4.6).

The New Corporate Marketer: Creating a Value Intelligence ABM Approach to Sponsorships

Earlier we talked about our work helping a client justify its sponsorship of an upcoming Olympics—a potentially massive investment. The engagement was successful, but it also highlighted how an AI-driven value management program could have ensured that the client achieved its lofty revenue goals.

Table 4.6:   Event/trade show booth AI use cases

#	ACTIVITY	SOURCE	AI-ASSISTED ACTIONS
1	Industry Value Intelligence Digital AI Expert	Internal product systems, value engineering systems, CRM, customer success systems	AI digital experts will support the booth staff, helping answer questions from participants related to their individual challenges (e.g., industry, function, geographical). The AI expert will provide a conversational experience that supports objection handling, recommends existing content to demonstrate customer success, industry thought leadership, and even recommend partners or other experts to help accelerate the buyer journey.
2	Participant AI Digital Concierge	Value engineering systems, CRM, customer success systems	As described earlier, the AI digital concierge can help schedule time with the right employees at the booth to answer specific questions.

Here's how:

1. The corporate event marketing team would develop value intelligence-based, event-specific product content, tools, and use cases, helping educate customers on how they can generate additional revenues from supporting the event. Similar AI-generated use cases would support product market positioning, pricing, promotions, and customer reference management activities.

2. Using an ABM-based strategy powered by a value intelligence, the event marketing team would use an AI assistant to educate sales teams on specific event solutions, target those customers impacted by the event, and manage and track progress against sales goals set for the event.

3. Marketers would create an AI assistant that tracks the incremental revenues generated from the event. This is key to providing visibility into the ROI of the event and allows for timely course corrections throughout the life cycle of the sponsorship.

Generative AI will play a pivotal role in making these activities happen quickly and cost-effectively. Table 4.7 summarizes use cases that help B2B corporate marketing teams maximize the performance of corporate sponsorships.

Table 4.7:   Corporate marketing assistant event use cases

	ACTIVITY	SOURCE	AI-ASSISTED ACTIONS
1	Event Solution Product Marketing Assistant	Product systems, partner systems, web, third-party research sources	Auto-generate event-specific value intelligence solution positioning content.
2	Event Digital Sales Assistant	Web, internal event content, solution assets	Use retrieval augmented generation (RAG) to answer questions about event details (timing, geographies, company sponsorship details, internal updates, solution messaging).
3	Event Ops Management Digital Analyst	CRM systems, sales systems	Automatically generate reporting related to prospect event discussions, bookings, billings, and recommendations related to: ▪ Solution messaging refinement ▪ Customer targeting ▪ Sales/partner engagement
4	Event Performance Reporting Analyst	Notes/ spreadsheets	Translate spreadsheet data into structured templates for analysis of: ▪ Costs ▪ Benefits ▪ Data gathering ▪ ROI model ▪ Metrics before and after

Smarter marketing investments

In the years ahead, we believe corporate marketing will need to justify the ROI of large corporate marketing investments to the board of directors and CFO. From event and sports team sponsorships to large advertising campaigns, the increasing adoption of AI solutions will help businesses better monitor and measure the impact of these high-profile investments. Moreover, it will create a more integrated and coordinated approach to managing and tracking investment results. In the end, it will allow CEOs and boards to more confidently invest in these strategic corporate marketing initiatives knowing that the results will be reported accurately and that course corrections will be quickly executed to increase investment success.

In the next chapter, we will move from the top of the marketing funnel where new leads are captured to the middle of the funnel—the province of sales and value management teams, where leads are converted into revenue. We will look at how sales, in concert with marketing and other departments, can reimagine and retool its organization with the help of value management strategies augmented by AI.

AI-Driven Value Management for Sales

Chapter 4, "AI-Driven Value Management for Marketing," discussed how value intelligence is critical to corporate, product, and revenue marketing programs as they craft strategies to build awareness, generate leads, and woo prospects. In this chapter, we will move further along the customer life cycle, where sales organizations convert these leads into opportunities and deals. If value intelligence is important to enhancing the effectiveness of marketing, it is at the very core of the sales process. This chapter explores the value management journey in sales organizations, how they build their teams and infrastructure, and the challenges they face. We will then look at ways AI can help overcome these challenges and recommend AI-based solutions.

A company's value proposition—whether or not it is formally articulated as a business case—lies at the center of all customer conversations that sellers have. Through the customer life cycle, sellers have an ongoing need to articulate business value—whether it is in building awareness for new products and services, seeking or enhancing relationships, responding to opportunities, or justifying a renewal. It is not surprising, therefore, that sales organizations tend to be one of the earliest and most enthusiastic adopters of value management among all the functions in a company.

Value management for sales begins with a formal business case, which is presented as an investment justification to help customers secure funding for the project. Numerous surveys reinforce the intuitive belief that good business cases are instrumental in ensuring deal wins for vendors. According to a recent study by Gong,[1] two-thirds of B2B buyers say that when sellers make their ROI case clear, it has a high influence on the likelihood to purchase. Many buyers will in fact insist on a business case for any investment greater than $50,000. We can use the customer-value life cycle, familiar to us from previous chapters, to better understand the scope of the sales organization's responsibilities (see Figure 5.1).

Scope of Value Management for Sales
Value Management Steps × Customer Life Cycle × Functional Activity

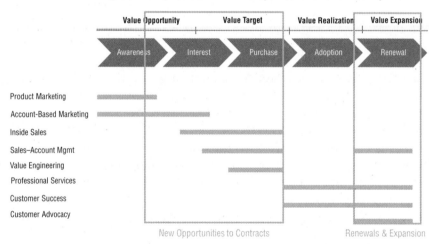

Figure 5.1: Sales' value management responsibilities across the customer life cycle

Put in simple terms, sales organizations own the Value Target and Expansion phases—that is, they are responsible for managing pipeline, closing new deals, securing renewals, and creating expansion opportunities. Sales teams are also focused on related outcomes such as increasing

---

[1] www.rainsalestraining.com/blog/4-misconceptions-of-making-a-strong-roi-case.

share of wallet, deal margins, customer satisfaction, and reducing churn. Note that sellers also take part in the Awareness or the Value Opportunity phase, which is traditionally owned by the marketing function for generating qualified leads for the business. As we discussed in Chapter 4, sellers and marketers collaborate through *account-based marketing (ABM)* approaches that can deliver game-changing results when executed effectively.

Let's follow the growth journey of a sales organization from the early stages of the company to enterprise-scale maturity. Along the way we will look at how value management programs are implemented, explore traditional approaches to scaling the program and the challenges faced, and how AI-driven value management can help you overcome the scaling challenges.

Getting Started with Value Management for Sales in Start-Ups and Small Companies

Most sales organizations make an early investment in value selling even when the company is in its infancy. Value selling is a sales approach that has a striking resemblance to the core concepts of value management, particularly in its focus on understanding and addressing the customer's needs by highlighting how the product or service can solve specific problems, improve the customer's situation, or deliver measurable benefits— all of which are aimed at creating a compelling reason for the customer to make a purchase. Value selling is a multidimensional operation in its own right, as described in many books, including Julie Thomas's *The Power of Value Selling: The Gold Standard to Drive Revenue and Create Customers for Life* (Wiley, 2023). Value selling can be an important first step in the journey to full value management capabilities.

Small companies and start-ups may have modest goals such as training their account executives and pre-sales consultants to create simple translations of features into benefits. If the technology product requires a nuanced value narrative that is more than just cost arbitrage, a dedicated value management practice will be required. Because of their demanding sales responsibilities, account executives and pre-sales teams will seldom have the bandwidth to create sophisticated value models and conduct business cases for each deal.

Just as customers need the help of solution consulting or pre-sales teams to propose the right product architecture and configuration, they also need value management teams to help understand the business value of the product and how it aligns with their strategic objectives. As the company grows, the need for advanced business cases with strategic and financial acumen arises, so it hires value management consultants to address this need. Their core skills in articulating business value not only helps win deals, but also secures renewals, creates new upsell opportunities, and generates new pipeline.

To help you understand what nascent value management programs look like *without AI*, we will explore the challenges companies face in building the capabilities, deal coverage, and customer outcomes they need to thrive and grow in this early phase, and will point out those areas AI can help fix.

Building VM Capabilities with People: Small, High-Powered Team Focused on Top Deals

During these initial stages, a handful of value management consultants are hired, and they take on the responsibility to develop value models and support deals with business cases. Early successes are critical. For most sales organizations at this stage, only a fraction of their deals is covered by this small value management team. The first few consultants take on the responsibility to deliver the proof of concept and establish the foundation for expanding the team.

> **VM PRO TIP**
>
> The first few value consultants are typically housed within the pre-sales or solution consulting organization. This is a great place to start your value management practice due to the common goals and engagement models shared by the two practices.

Building VM Capabilities with Process: Manual Value Management Programs

In these early stages of the company's journey, the investment in a value management program is obviously small and thus begins with a small business value team. There is not much of a process or technology infrastructure available to support the work of value consultants. Planning is done through spreadsheets and emails, and creating business cases is almost fully manual, supported with spreadsheets and slide presentations. Key tasks include the following:

Value Model Development   Value consultants spend time creating value models that define how product features are translated into business capabilities and outcomes. This process takes weeks of collaboration with the product team. There is little automation to help streamline model development, which is typically done in spreadsheets.

Operating Model Development   Given the small size of the team, operating models or governance mechanisms are not yet in place. Decisions on which deals will get business case support are made by the sales and solution consulting leadership, generally based on deal size.

Business Case Creation   As you can imagine, value management consultants spend a lot of time conducting research and analysis, building models, creating collaborative business cases, and undertaking customer engagements in support of opportunities. The ability to cover deal opportunities is limited by the capacity of the value engineering team.

VM PRO TIP

Developing business cases should be a collaborative effort of the account executive, solution consultant, value consultant—and the customer. The customer's role is not just to provide all the data required. The best business cases are created when you get the customer's executives to "own" the business case and feel invested in it. This ensures continual engagement of the customer at every step of the engagement and invariably results in a stronger and more successful case study.

Much of the work of creating a business case is manual, tedious, and difficult to automate. Let's look at some of the challenges organizations face at these early stages, as detailed in Table 5.1.

Table 5.1:   Business case effort decomposition

TYPE OF BUSINESS CASE	TASKS AND CHALLENGES
Customer value hypothesis (Early sales stages when customer involvement is low or nonexistent) Uses publicly available information and document research to create an outside-in business case	Each manual task listed may take between a few hours to a few days per business case, depending on the size and complexity of the deal ▪ Industry and company research on the web ▪ Customer research via 10-K and annual reports
Customer value assessment (Later sales stages when customer involvement is high) Uses customer-provided information and extensive collaboration and validation to create a detailed *customer value assessment*. Requires multiple interviews with the customer, socialization of the results, and iterations/refinement to gain approvals	▪ Synthesizing customer discovery meeting notes and recordings ▪ Value analysis with spreadsheets ▪ Doing what-if ROI scenarios ▪ Preparing the final deliverable
Customer value road map (Later sales stages when customer involvement is high, and a technical road map needs to be presented) Goes beyond the customer value assessment to define a *strategic road map* that shows how the value will be realized. This requires close collaboration between the solution consultant and the customer's technical team	

Building VM Capabilities with Technology: Value Automation Platforms Can Increase Business Case Productivity

Once the value models are developed, value automation platforms can be implemented to simplify and streamline the creation of customer business cases. These tools encode the ROI model and templates for communicating the strategic alignment of the product to customer objectives. They automate certain parts of the process and standardize the way business cases are done, while saving time. These platforms typically integrate with CRM systems to create a seamless workflow for the sales teams.

Building Deal Coverage and Customer Outcomes

Naturally, at this early stage, coverage of deals and accounts is limited. In terms of outcomes, delivering a value consultant proof of concept is a good way to start—and you can prove the ROI of the program by demonstrating its impact on win rates and time to close deals, and accelerating the sales conversation with compelling value narratives.

Figure 5.2 shows how the value management practice can be summarized at this early stage in the company's growth.

Value Management Starter Kit

Capability	**People:** A few value management consultants (1–5) work on handpicked deals as proof of concept, while laying out the framework for a larger practice.
	Process: No formal value management process or governance. Deals are supported with formal business cases led by consultants ("hi-touch" engagement). Business case creation is largely manual.
	Technology: Basic value automation for ROI modeling but digitization of customer value engagements, or integration with CRM.
Coverage	**Sales Deal Support:** Very limited coverage of a fraction of deals given the high manual nature of performing a business case project and limited value engineering resources.
Customer Outcomes	**Sales Impact:** Early deal wins influenced by value management consultants serve as proof of concept. Value models for products are developed.

Figure 5.2: Value Management Starter Kit & Maturity Assessment

With a few business cases now under its belt, the business value team can demonstrate their impact on deal wins to sales leaders. It is now time to expand the team to cover more products, accounts, and deals.

Next, we'll take a look at how, as the company grows, the team scales the value program to achieve more coverage of deals and drive revenue influence with more investments in people, process, and technology.

HOW AI START-UP CRON AI EXPLAINS THE ART OF THE POSSIBLE TO ITS CUSTOMERS

Cron AI is a start-up that provides 3D perception and visual intelligence solutions for machines and infrastructures across industries. Cron AI's flagship offering, senseEDGE, aims to bring contextual awareness to machines, enabling them to perceive and understand the environment in three dimensions, which is crucial for building autonomous systems in industries ranging from transportation systems and data center security to industrial automation and robotics.

Recently we met with Tushar Chhabra, the CEO and cofounder of Cron AI, to talk about how he and his team are articulating the value of the solutions they offer. His company's senseEDGE solution is earning a reputation as a game changer in the industry, using AI-powered algorithms to provide extreme accuracy in interpreting LiDAR (light detection and ranging) data in real time. Cron AI's products not only solve companies' existing problems better, faster, and cheaper, but they open a whole new set of business opportunities—enabling what you might call the "art of the possible."

The company is seeing early success in deploying value selling to help customers imagine and understand these new possibilities. For example, in the intelligent transportation systems market, sales teams are proving Cron AI's potential to reduce traffic congestion by 40 percent and the carbon footprint by 30 percent. What's more, its product can unearth previously unavailable intelligence to vastly improve traffic management efficiency.

Chhabra told us it takes a lot of teamwork between product and sales teams to develop these use cases, tailor them for the industry and the customer, and present them in an engaging and compelling manner. It is here that his company can be challenged by resource and talent shortages. Not surprisingly, this AI innovator recognizes it can greatly benefit from a combination of predictive and generative AI to help create these sophisticated value narratives with customers.

From Art to Craft to Practice: How Value Management Programs Support Mature Sales Organizations

As these initial business cases start driving deal wins and pipeline, sales organizations look for ways to expand the team of value consultants, aiming to cover more products, deals, and accounts, and achieve revenue benefits at scale.

Let's now examine mature value management programs *without AI*, identify the challenges companies confront at this stage, and point out those areas AI can help fix.

Building VM Capabilities with People: Creating an Independent Function for Value Management

The business value team at this stage has typically grown from just a few consultants to anywhere between 10 and 100+ consultants, depending on the size of the business. Organizationally, a dedicated business value practice is created as an entity separate from the solution consulting organization and is focused on scaling up the success that they achieved during the start-up phase of value management.

THE HIGH VALUE OF VALUE ENGINEERS

Hiring value consultants is an expensive proposition, and it limits the number of consultants in the team. There are several reasons for this: (1) Consultants need to have the experience and gravitas to call on the executive level of your customer. (2) They need to be industry or solution experts to build the detailed ROI models. (3) They need consultative skills to be able to build custom business cases for their most strategic customers. Depending on the experience level, a value consultant can cost between $200,000 and $500,000 per year.

"A great value engineer needs to bring a confluence of skills, from management consulting to financial analytics, to technical knowledge, to executive communications and sales," says Paul Randlesome, value management leader at HPE Aruba Networking. Given their unique expertise, finding experienced candidates can be difficult. According to Randlesome, "Value engineers manage our most high-visibility deals, speaking with the C-level audience at our customers and often interacting with our senior leadership."

Randlesome's experience is typical for value engineering programs at large organizations. It's why these talented individuals are best focused on cultivating strong partnerships with their organization's most strategic customers.

RATIO OF VALUE CONSULTANTS TO ACCOUNT EXECUTIVES

At this stage, the staffing levels of the value management team may approach the headcount ratios of already mature practices like solution consultants, which can be as high as one consultant for every account executive. As the business value team reaches this staffing level, managers and program support staff will also need to be hired, which increases the overhead to run the function.

As we have discussed before, creating a successful business case is a team effort spearheaded by the value consultant but with active participation from the account executive and the solution consultant. With the expansion of the business value team, there is now a need for standardizing the way this orchestration is done. Roles and responsibilities must be defined for each contributor—namely, the account executive and solution consultant—as they support the value consultant. These are detailed in Table 5.2.

Table 5.2: Business case responsibilities

ROLE	BUSINESS CASE RESPONSIBILITIES
Value Consultant	Responsible for presenting to the CxO at the customer; business case owner
	Collaborates with the customer to collect data specific for measuring the benefits and ensuring executive buy-in for the assumptions in the model
	Works with the account executive and solution consultant to model the investment requirements (e.g., bill of materials, services, discounts) and the timing of the investment (e.g., rollout plan)
Account Executive	Reviews account plan and share customer objectives and strategies with the value management consultant
	Provides perspective on the account, existing opportunities, buying centers, and areas for value creation
	Makes introductions to customer stakeholders
	Reviews business case content
Solution Consultant	Helps the value management consultant understand how the solution is architected, the capabilities it delivers for the customer, and how the solution works
	Reviews and validates that value claims are credible given the underlying capabilities

Each of the team members brings specific skills to guide the value conversation with the customer. As we have seen from our experiences with these teams, a typical headcount distribution for the three roles can be such that a value consultant can support up to 10 account executives and the solution consultants can support up to three account executives (see Figure 5.3). Typically for enterprise B2B companies, the account executive will be dedicated to one customer. As you move down to a second customer tier (sometimes called commercial accounts), these account executives may have multiple customers, but they also are leaned on to perform their own business cases.

	Sales Mindset	Product Knowledge	Solution Architect	Basic Value Selling	Advanced Financial Modeling	Strategy Consulting
Account Executives	☑	☑		☑		
Solution Architects (3–5 per Account Executive)	☑	☑	☑	☑		
Value Engineers (10–12 per Account Executive)	☑	☑	☑	☑	☑	☑

Figure 5.3: Business case skills by role and distribution

WHAT DOES SUCCESS LOOK LIKE? A TECH INVESTOR WEIGHS IN

San Francisco–based Ridge Ventures specializes in early-stage investments, focusing on innovative technology start-ups, providing strategic guidance, and supporting growth through its extensive network and expertise. We recently asked Yousuf Khan, a partner at Ridge, to share his perspective on the high-tech space and how vendors can connect with customers with a value management approach. Khan has more than 20 years of experience as a CIO, adviser, and investor in the enterprise software space.

Khan has one key piece of advice for technology vendors: "It's not always just about ROI," he says. "I get the ROI and the dollars. I get the features and the capabilities. But ultimately, the question I ask is, what does success look like?" He says there are three ways to answer that question: (1) by providing exceptional clarity on solving the business problem you originally wanted to solve for, (2) by providing a very clear target of what *good* looks like, and (3) by demonstrating how your solution fits into the customer's technology and business architecture.

"Connecting the dots from the customer's problem to your solution is important," he stresses. When Khan was a CIO of Pure Storage, he spent a lot of time not just doing IT but also working with his customers speaking CIO-to-CIO, helping them understand how the company's storage solutions can help solve their business problems. For example, he explained how an agile, fast data management system can prevent downtime—a crucial capability in a business where even a few hours of downtime can wipe out your wafer-thin margins.

Khan says that vendors often miss the importance of aligning to the customer's business and collaborating with the customer in helping it realize business value. "How curious is the vendor about the customer's industry and business? If you look deeper into the vendor's organization and their competencies, ask yourself if they have invested in vertical or industry expertise so that they can speak the language of the customer. Value is a multidimensional thing. It takes a lot of knowledge orchestration to get all this done," he says.

Building VM Capabilities with Technology: Enabling VM at Scale

The value management program at this stage requires a substantial amount of investment in technology to support the work of a large team of value consultants, digitize workflows, and drive productivity. The technology infrastructure will require CRM enhancements, analytics, value automation tools, and knowledge management solutions.

- **CRM system:** The CRM system is not only used for managing accounts and opportunities but also to track value management customer engagements. A number of enhancements can be made to the system to accommodate specific needs such as connecting an engagement to multiple opportunities or connecting an account to multiple engagements and its deliverable documents.

- **Value automation platform:** As described in the previous section, value automation platforms are business case development tools. Business cases developed using the platform can be connected to the CRM system to provide a unified experience.

- **CRM analytics:** These solutions help answer various queries on accounts, opportunities, and engagements to help provide both leading and lagging indicators of engagement status, coverage levels, and outcomes influenced. This is an essential tool for both short- and long-term planning for resource deployment and engagement planning.

- **Knowledge management (KM) systems:** KM systems are a vital part of a value management practice. A wealth of knowledge is gathered in each customer engagement, including knowledge about the industry, the company, and relevant data on opportunities, engagements, and business case deliverables. These need to be available for efficient search and retrieval to promote knowledge sharing and ideation.

Building VM Capabilities with Process: Organization, Governance, and Operating Models Struggle Under Their Own Weight

Even with structured roles, standardized processes, and technology automation tools in place, much of the core business case creation work is still manual, tedious, and difficult to automate. Table 5.3 shows the collection of tasks and challenges most companies face when building the typical business case.

Table 5.3:   Putting together the pieces of a business case

TYPE OF BUSINESS CASE	TASKS/CHALLENGE
Customer value hypothesis (Early sales stages when customer involvement is low or nonexistent) Uses publicly available information and document research to create an *outside-in business case*	Each manual task listed takes between *a few hours to a few days per business case*, depending on the size and complexity of the deal ■ Industry and company research on the web ■ Customer research via 10K/annual reports
Customer value assessment (Later sales stages when customer involvement is high) Uses customer-provided information and extensive collaboration and validation to create a detailed *customer value assessment*	■ CRM structured data analysis on opportunities and accounts ■ CRM unstructured data analysis on timelines/notes ■ Synthesizing customer discovery meeting notes and recordings
Customer value road map (Later sales stages when customer involvement is high, and a technical road map needs to be presented) Goes beyond the customer value assessment to define a *strategic road map* to success to define *how* the value will be realized. This requires close collaboration with the solution consultant and the customer's technical team	■ Value analysis with spreadsheets ■ Doing what-if ROI scenarios ■ Preparing the final deliverable

Value Model Development

Value consultants continue to spend time updating value models as new product features are launched, but the effort is more organized and collaborative than in the initial stages. Agreements are made with the product marketing team to collaboratively build value intelligence assets, including the model for business cases. They work together to ensure proper training for the sales team as well as the other value management consultants on the usage of these new value models, ensuring they are ready for use at the time of product launch.

Engagement Planning

With an expanded operation, on any given day, the most important questions for a business value team in a sales organization are questions like "Which new deals require value consulting support?" and "Which deal needs urgent help?" These can be complex questions to answer because of the significant number of variables that may need to be considered. Particularly in large operations, value consultants and their managers may spend hours to days doing this manually. What adds to the complexity is that the landscape of opportunities may change every single day.

Administration and Reporting

With a CRM system and analytics platform enhanced to support value management activities, and a value automation tool in place, routine administrative tasks such as creating monthly reports can become noticeably easier, but engagement updates still require manual efforts. Any custom report needs to be developed to answer questions about the account, opportunities, and engagements.

We'll cover how AI addresses engagement planning, administration, and reporting challenges in our next chapter, "AI for Sales Operations."

Training and Content Development

Business value teams typically spend several days in a quarter dedicated to the creation of content for training the sales team to help them self-service or create their own business cases.

HOW LEADERBOARDS CAN DRIVE ADOPTION AND BUILD BUSINESS CASE MUSCLE

One of the top enterprise software companies implemented a "high-touch and low-touch" operating model to optimize its deployment of value management consultants. Value management consultants would support large and complex deals above a certain threshold deal size. For all other deals below this threshold, account executives and solution consultants (referred to as sellers) would create their own business cases. They would go through quarterly enablement programs led by value management consultants where they would develop and hone their ability to create their own business cases. Value management consultants would also hold "office hours" to answer questions and provide coaching.

This model took a while to produce results, since it took time to ensure all account executives and solution consultants were trained in creating business cases. Adoption was driven through gamifying the percentage of deals for which sellers created on their own. Leaderboards and awards became a popular part of quarterly business reviews. Within two quarters, however, sales teams started closing more deals successfully through this two-tiered approach.

Organization

As soon as the team grows beyond a handful of value consultants, it becomes necessary to make investments to organize them efficiently into a separate organization with managers and program office investments. Additional investments in travel and administrative support are necessary for alignment with sales teams and geographies.

Operating Model and Demand Management

Ad hoc decisions may work when the team is small, but as it grows, roles, responsibilities and workflows should be defined for how business value services will work on the ground. Value consultants will need to spend time on the planning and orchestration required to operate this model on the ground. Due to the excessive cost of value consultants, it makes sense that these consultants focus on the largest deals so that there is maximum return on the investment. Deal size thresholds may be defined so that the value management consultant's efforts can be concentrated on the most important, large, and complex deals and accounts. This would leave the rest for account executives and pre-sales teams to self-service their own business case needs.

In reality, though, there is always a large number of strategic accounts and deals that do not get the necessary high-touch consultant-led engagement. Here's why:

- Deal volume is difficult to predict particularly during busy quarters, resulting in uneven workloads.

- Some business cases take an inordinate amount of time due to excessively tedious manual work.

- Capacity is taken up due to engagement in small deals because sales teams demand it. They see potential for pipeline growth. Note that value management consultants also can help sales teams generate new pipeline through consultative "art of the possible" perspectives they can develop for customers. This type of engagement is critical for realizing the full revenue potential from accounts in which there may not be potential for large deals considering the limited relationship with the customer's senior leadership.

THE TYPICAL WORKLOAD FOR VALUE MANAGEMENT CONSULTANTS

The number of large and complex deals a value management consultant can support with business cases or customer engagements quarter varies across companies, but our experience is that you should expect a value consultant to hit their maximum capacity at 7–10 engagements per quarter.

While these programmatic investments do have an impact in driving productivity, the core work of creating a business case continues to involve a large number of manual and tedious tasks. It is here that AI holds vast potential to create efficiencies.

Improving Deal Coverage and Customer Outcomes

In an ideal world, sales teams would prefer to have value management coverage for at least the top 50 percent of deals and top accounts, representing 50 percent of the company's revenue potential. But the budget required for this is extremely high. What we learned from the pre-AI era experience of helping build successful value management programs in companies like Salesforce, ServiceNow, Oracle, and Cisco is that scaling business value teams is a resource-intensive, long-term project. It can cost millions of dollars and years to mature a value management program with the right mix of people, process, and technologies.

Together, these challenges limit the productivity of the business value team. Put differently, to increase revenue outcomes, more expensive consultants would need to be hired. It is at this stage that most companies get stuck. On the one hand, they know the business value team is delivering benefits such as enhanced pipeline and revenue expansion. But on the other hand, scaling the team requires hiring more consultants and often hits a budget wall. In fact, without enabling processes and technology, the benefits do not even scale in a linear fashion. Some companies may have tens of millions of dollars and resources available to solve for this, but most do not.

Figure 5.4 illustrates how we can summarize this stage, whether it is a medium-sized or large-sized value management operation.

Capability	**People:** A few value management consultants (1–5) work on handpicked deals as proof of concept, while laying out the framework for a larger practice	
	Process: No formal value management process or governance. Deals are supported with formal business cases led by consultants ("hi-touch" engagement). Business case creation is largely manual.	
	Technology: Basic value automation for ROI modeling but digitization of customer value engagements, or integration with CRM	
Coverage	**Sales Deal Support:** Very limited coverage of a fraction of deals given the high manual nature of performing a business case project and limited value engineering resources	
Customer Outcomes	**Sales Impact:** Early deal wins influenced by value management consultants serve as proof of concept. Value models for products are developed	

Figure 5.4: Business value teams—current state of enterprise deployment

We have seen how process and technology initiatives can drive productivity improvements to a certain extent, but large parts of business case creation and engagement management remain manual. The central question therefore is how to automate these "knowledge-based" tasks using AI. Let's now explore how AI can help solve them to create AI-driven value management organization of the future.

What's Next: AI-Driven Value Management for Sales

A combination of predictive and generative AI capabilities can be deployed to address many of the challenges mentioned in the previous section. To define the most impactful use cases for AI-driven value management for sales, let's look at some of the core capabilities AI brings to the table and their potential uses in the sales journey (Table 5.4).

Table 5.4: AI capabilities for sales use cases

AI CAPABILITY	POTENTIAL USE CASES
Prediction algorithms	Forecasting of value management revenue influence in upcoming quarters
Deal scoring	Determination of business case support for opportunities

Continues

Table 5.4: (*continued*)

AI CAPABILITY	POTENTIAL USE CASES
Text summarization	Summarization of customer meeting notes from CRM and emails
Sentiment analysis	Customer sentiment analysis based on emails and CRM timeline notes
Document Q&A	Customer or industry document queries
Audio transcripts	Customer meeting transcripts
Data visualization	ROI analysis and business case deliverable preparation
Translation	Translation of working documents and outputs for cross-language collaboration
Research	Industry and company research as part of account planning and business cases
Database Q&A	Deal, account and engagement queries of the CRM system
Automated workflows	Automatic engagement creation based on deal/account variables

We believe these AI capabilities can be deployed in B2B businesses today to solve many of the challenges faced by value management programs, providing new levels of efficiencies, scalability, and sales success. Let's now look at each of those capabilities.

Introducing the AI-Powered Value Consultant

Foundation models such as Open AI's GPT-4, or o1 and Google's Gemini can be leveraged along with traditional applications to develop AI assistants for value consultants. These AI assistants can be trained in value management taxonomy and concepts, as well as business case templates. Unstructured and structured data involved in business case development as well as engagement planning can now be processed by AI assistants. This capability adds much-needed capacity at a much lower cost to boost the productivity of the team, their coverage of deals and accounts, as well as outcomes (see Table 5.5).

Table 5.5: AI value consultant digital assistant

CHALLENGE	SOLUTION	TECHNOLOGY COMPONENTS
Consultants are expensive to hire	Develop AI assistants that can augment consultant capacity	▪ Foundation models (from OpenAI/Google) ▪ Database ▪ Application layer ▪ User interface ▪ APIs

AI Technology: Powering Up Value Management Platforms

AI can help companies derive more value from the existing value management technology infrastructure that we described in the current state of value management programs.

- **CRM:** AI can help answer complex queries to the CRM database and conduct correlation analysis on opportunity and engagement data. This can be a game-changing capability for value management since they are always looking to optimally deploy resources. Questions such as, "Which new deals require value management support?" or "Which deal needs urgent help?" have vast contextual dependence and used to take extensive report development customization to be able to answer without the help of large language models (LLM). AI can usher in a new era of agility and data-driven decision-making for the management of engagements.

- **Value automation:** AI can help structure and synthesize input data required for the tool, as well as query relevant business case data through APIs to answer specific questions and perform what-if analyses on ROI scenarios.

- **Analytics:** AI can turn plain language questions into analytics and reports, leveraging resources like sales databases, value automation tools, and knowledge repositories. This approach not only reduces development time but also enhances the user experience.

For many of the manual activities performed by account executives, value consultants, and solution consultants today, the value consultant digital assistant can take these tasks off their plate. Table 5.6 highlights how the digital assistant can automate these tasks.

Table 5.6:   AI capabilities for value management account activities

CHALLENGE	SOLUTION	TECHNOLOGY COMPONENTS
It takes hours and sometimes days to: ■ Prepare account and opportunity summary; query CRM system for data related to accounts, opportunities, and engagements ■ Perform correlation analysis on accounts, opportunities, and engagements	Develop AI assistants trained to understand standard queries, translate and run SQL type queries to retrieve the required results Run code interpretation on CRM data to provide aggregate results from data sets	■ Foundation models (from OpenAI/Google) ■ Database ■ Application layer ■ User interface ■ APIs ■ Custom AI development using assistants or agentic AI

AI-Enhanced Processes: Exponentially Scaling Value Management Programs

From building business cases faster and more accurately to generating content and training courses in minutes, AI-driven processes can help automate manual and repetitive tasks and save hours of time while reducing errors.

Business Case Creation

Much of the manual and tedious work that is required today to perform a business case can now be taken on by AI. In Tables 5.7 and 5.8, we detail how the AI solution addresses this challenge and the specific use cases it will support.

Table 5.7:   AI process automation for business cases

CHALLENGE	SOLUTION	TECHNOLOGY COMPONENTS
Each manual task listed takes between *a few hours to a few days per business case*, depending on the size and complexity of the deal. ▪ Industry and company research on the web ▪ Customer research via 10-K/annual reports ▪ CRM structured data analysis on opportunities and accounts ▪ CRM unstructured data analysis on timelines/notes ▪ Synthesizing customer discovery meeting notes and recordings ▪ Value analysis with spreadsheets ▪ Doing what-if ROI scenarios	Develop AI assistants trained to understand the language and structure of business cases, including discovery, strategy map development, and ROI analysis Please see Table 5.8 for a more detailed breakdown	▪ Foundation models (from OpenAI/Google) ▪ Database ▪ Application layer ▪ App user interface/chatbot UI ▪ APIs with CRM and value automation tool ▪ Custom AI development using assistants or agentic AI

Table 5.8:   Key use cases for AI digital assistants

#	ACTIVITY	SOURCE	AI-ASSISTED ACTIONS
1	Industry research	Web	Automatically place an API call to free or paid subscription sites to retrieve, structure, and summarize industry trends, priorities, and news
2	Customer research	10-K/annual report Company website CRM	Use retrieval augmented generation (RAG) to answer questions about company 10-Ks to summarize company priorities

Continues

Table 5.8: (*continued*)

#	ACTIVITY	SOURCE	AI-ASSISTED ACTIONS
3	Customer discovery	Meeting notes and recordings	Act as a meeting transcriber. Structure meeting notes in predetermined templates ■ Business objectives/priorities ■ Problems/opportunities being addressed ■ Solution under consideration ■ Use cases and capabilities
4	Value analysis	Notes/ spreadsheets	Translate spreadsheet data into structured templates for analysis ■ Costs ■ Benefits ■ Data gathering ■ ROI model ■ Metrics before and after
5	Business objectives and capabilities summary	All of the above	Summarize, synthesize, and structure value assessment results into predetermined templates ■ ROI results ■ Use cases before and after ■ Financial and strategic benefits summary
7	Final deliverable	All of the above	Produce draft of final presentation deliverable

ELEVATING THE CUSTOMER CONVERSATION WITH AI

How has today's ultra-fast-moving markets impacted the competitive landscape for technology vendors? A lot, says Yousuf Khan, a partner at Ridge Ventures.

"You know, there are 50 start-ups being born during the 30 minutes we've had this conversation. It is much easier to create a product than ever before. There's competition! Leading with value in this multidimensional way is the only way to differentiate yourself."

Yousuf sees a huge upside for B2B enterprises that recognize AI's potential. "With AI, companies that 'get it' can now implement it by bringing knowledge and expertise across functions to the customer conversation," he says. For the first time, he sees companies achieving what he calls "analysis at scale."

Training and Content Development: Autogenerating Content for Value Management Programs

Content generation is one of the most widely used capabilities of generative AI. AI assistants can help value management teams save several days' worth of effort every quarter by rapidly generating content to help sales teams create own business cases on their own. We summarize how AI can autogenerate this training content in Table 5.9.

Table 5.9:   AI capabilities for value management training content

CHALLENGE	SOLUTION	TECHNOLOGY COMPONENTS
Value management consultants spend hours helping account executives and solution consultants develop business cases	Develop AI assistants that can answer questions, provide coaching, and show examples	■ Foundation models (from OpenAI/Google) with extensive custom-developed prompts ■ Application layer ■ User interface ■ APIs

A Quantum Leap in Coverage and Customer Outcomes Using AI

Regardless of where you are in your value management journey, an AI-driven value management program can provide a significant uplift to deal coverage and outcomes. In combination with the right mix of people, process, and technology, AI can boost pipeline, close more deals, and drive upsells and renewals for the sales organization throughout the customer life cycle.

As shown in Figure 5.5, increasing AI capabilities and deal coverage can add a boost to customer outcomes—and thus drive revenue—in each phase of the life cycle.

AI-VM programs will be a game changer for sales organizations, empowering them to scale expensive value consulting resources by increasing their productivity twofold or greater; helping drive more value from their existing sales technologies; and enabling account executives to build business cases faster than ever before while enhancing training content and delivery. All of these advancements combined will allow organizations to break down the current barriers we see in value management programs today. Figure 5.6 summarizes the impact of AI-VM for sales organizations.

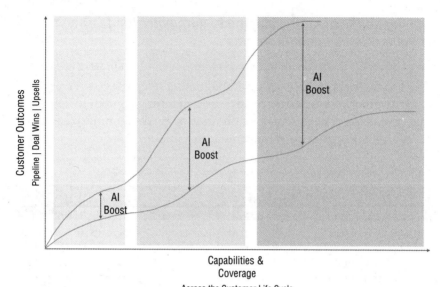

Figure 5.5: Quantum leap in ability to scale value management

Value Management—AI-VM Enabled Sales

Capability	**People:** Full value management practice with consultants and AI assistants organized into a separate team, aligned to sales teams. 2X capacity without having to hire the headcount; AI assistants act as coaches for account executives and solution consultants. **Process:** Formal value management process or governance supported by AI-led planning and agility. Business case development is AI-assisted.
Coverage	**Technology:** AI integrated into CRM, analytics, and value automation **Sales Deal Support:** All deals requiring business cases are supported by value consulting digital assistants. The AI digital assistant helps to scale value consultants capacity by 2x +, increasing their coverage and reducing costs and account executives can perform business cases with value consulting digital assistant support.
Customer Outcomes	**Sales Impact:** 2X pipeline, 2X deal wins, and 2X upsells.

Figure 5.6: AI-VM enabled value management for sales

Chapter 6, "AI for Sales Operations," will explore how AI can help with sales operations, which is critical not just for the success of the sales organization but also for the value management team.

AI for Sales Operations

After looking at value management for sales, let's turn our attention to the behind-the-scenes operations of the sales organization, which play a critical role in establishing key systems and processes and streamlining data management for both sales and business value teams.

The sales operations teams are often faced with complex challenges in supporting their sales teams. One common problem is simply keeping up with the breadth and dynamics of the solutions that the company sells. It's a never-ending, changing landscape, and the sales operations team needs to keep pace to ensure that the account teams are prepared with the latest product content, pricing, and promotions and understand the latest competitive landscape changes.

In addition, rapid turnover of sales reps and management can wear on the operations team. Just as they feel they've accomplished their goals to arm and prepare sales with the right go-to-market messaging and tools, new sales members are brought in to take over for resources that have left the company. As described in this chapter, an effective sales operations team that collaborates with the business value teams can drive significant revenue benefits.

Understanding the Responsibilities of the Sales Operations Team

The scope of sales operations can vary slightly from company to company, but here are some of the typical responsibilities they take on, specifically when it comes to collaborating with value management teams (Figure 6.1):

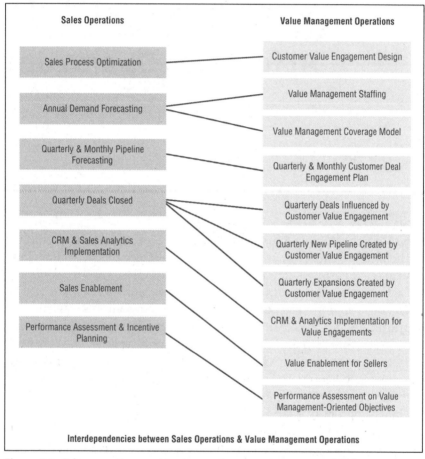

Figure 6.1: Sales operations and business value operations responsibilities

Sales Process Optimization   In enterprise-scale companies, the sales operations teams focus on streamlining and optimizing the sales process to improve efficiency and effectiveness. The effort extends to value management engagements, which are typically integrated into the sales process throughout the customer life cycle, from the initial awareness and interest phase to the purchase, adoption, and expansion phases.

Data Analysis and Reporting   Sales operations staff are tasked with analyzing sales data to identify trends, opportunities, and areas for improvement and with generating reports to aid decision-making. This is vital input for joint planning sessions between account executives and value consultants so that value assessment efforts can be focused on areas that require the most help from the highly skilled value consultants.

Sales Tools and Technology Management   Another area handled by sales operations staff is managing and optimizing sales tools and technologies, such as CRM systems to support sales team productivity and effectiveness. In most companies, value management workflows are also designed using the same CRM systems, creating a unified process for account teams. In addition, value automation tools may be involved in creating business cases as well as knowledge and content management systems to maintain a repository of historical content. All these tools and technologies need to work together seamlessly, and when they're deployed correctly, the sales teams shouldn't know where one platform starts or ends.

FROM SPREADSHEETS TO AI – BUILDING A BUSINESS INTELLIGENCE PROGRAM FOR VALUE CONSULTANTS

Sam Bouhdary wears many hats. He's an art entrepreneur turned business intelligence expert and program manager. His specialty is building applications for sales, solution consulting, and value management teams. Bouhdary focuses on getting the right data and insights to sellers so they can close deals faster.

"It's all about helping them focus on the right accounts and opportunities daily," Bouhdary says. "I used to pull sales data into spreadsheets and prep standard reports monthly." As the business grew, Bouhdary had to manage thousands of rows, then hundreds of thousands. "It was like steering a ship. Running quick scenarios like, 'What if I target only deals above $500K?' became impossible. We needed a better system."

Bouhdary led the design and rollout of an analytics dashboard that supported a multi-billion-dollar revenue stream. "We had to work with IT to show them the complexity of sales support. Sales uses the CRM for accounts and opportunities. Solution consulting and value management handle the same data, plus engagements."

Value management teams often have defined services, engagement workflows, and KPI tracking, Bouhdary's team needed to build all of that into the CRM for analytics. "It's like building an ERP for the value team," Bouhdary says. "Don't tell your IT team that—it's not your typical enhancement!"

Bouhdary's experience highlights the need for clear scope and understanding when building systems for sales support. It can be as complex as implementing CRM for sales, so planning is key. Value consultants also need content like business cases, so Bouhdary's team quickly built a knowledge management system.

"Six months in, we had a working dashboard with real-time coverage data, projections, and pre-formatted reports," Bouhdary says. This saved our consultants 20% of the time they'd spend looking for data or prepping for meetings with sales or customers."

But new requests kept coming. Consultants wanted filters for account type, territory, quarter, deal size, sales stage, product scope, and more. "I wondered—what if we had a system that could understand natural language, turn it into SQL, and get the answers consultants need? Like an AI chatbot."

This came at the right time, as GenAI was emerging as a capability to watch. Now, Bouhdary is working on building a GenAI-based system to do exactly that.

Forecasting and Pipeline Management   This is one of the most valuable activities for sales operations, providing direction and guidance to sales efforts to ensure accurate revenue projections and resource allocation. Over the last two decades, we have seen rapidly increasing use of data and data science solutions to develop sales forecasts and manage sales pipelines. Business value teams depend on accurate sales forecasting and pipeline management to direct their efforts to where it's required the most.

VM PRO TIP

Long-range plans (LRPs) are common in sales organizations as a way to make 1–3-year forecasts and arrive at both budgets and revenue targets. When the business value team is fully staffed to support the top accounts and deals, it is important that they also make long-range plans so that they can support these sales goals.

The sales operations team usually guides this exercise, acting as a "budget manager" or bridge between the sales team, the finance team, and support organizations such as solution consulting and value management.

Building an LRP can take months and several planning cycles, so you should initiate your LRP in the middle of the previous year to make sure the required headcount, technology, and other program budgets, operating models, as well as outcome targets are agreed upon.

Sales Performance Measurement   Establishing key performance indicators (KPIs) and metrics to measure sales team performance is one of the most important responsibilities of sales operations. In advanced value management programs, value-related KPIs may be part of sales' performance measurement. These indicators could include the adoption of value tools by sales regions, the number of business cases created by account executives on their own, or the percentage of deals supported by business cases.

Sales Training and Enablement   Sales operations staff provide sales teams with the training, resources, and support they need to succeed. This includes getting sales reps up to speed on value management concepts—not just in order to help them create their own business cases, but also to help them work effectively with the value consultants. Note that in many sales organizations, the enablement function may be separate from sales operations. For example, at Cisco, there is a dedicated training department.

VM PRO TIP

As you are growing your business value team, be sure to build a strong relationship with the sales operations group. This collaboration will serve as the foundation for developing the process and technology required for your team to scale. And as your business value team grows, sales operations can help you secure the right kind of attention needed to get involved in annual and quarterly sales planning—and, of course, secure the budgets required to scale your value management program.

Adding AI to Sales Operations to Quickly Scale Value Management Programs

As we described above effective sales operations team is critical to meeting the revenue goals of the company. Overcoming many of the common challenges faced by these operations teams has been challenging, and they are often solved by throwing more human resources (internal or contracting) at the problem. Now let's look at how we can deploy AI instead and how AI can better integrate operations, sales, and business value teams. Table 6.1 highlights the top AI sales operations use cases that we see driving productivity and cost savings.

Table 6.1:   AI sales operations use cases

AREA	CHALLENGE	HOW AI CAN HELP
Sales and value management process optimization	▪ Slow, manual processes in value engagement planning and orchestration ▪ Lack of visibility into process bottlenecks	▪ AI can help analyze historical sales and value engagement data to identify process improvements. ▪ If the workflows are digitized with CRM systems, generative AI can automate routine tasks, freeing up time for value management consultants and sales reps to focus on high-value deals and activities.
Data analysis and reporting	▪ Inefficient data silos across CRM, ERP, value automation, and incentive planning systems ▪ Data inaccuracy and incompleteness ▪ Insufficient leading indicators vs. lagging indicators	▪ With predictive AI, large volumes of data from disparate sources can be analyzed to uncover insights and trends to offer more leading indicators, such as deal win probability and revenue. ▪ Generative AI can augment this by generating reports automatically, ensuring accurate and timely reporting.
Sales and value tools and technology management	▪ Multiple systems are hard to manage ▪ Poor user adoption ▪ Integration challenges	▪ Value automation, CRM, and analytics tools require a lot of configuration and design work. AI solutions can analyze user behavior and preferences and provide inputs to optimize the design and functionality of value automation and sales tools. ▪ Once the workflows are digitized, generative AI can be used to automate data integration and streamline workflows across different systems. ▪ An example of this is the automated notification for a value consultant of a new sales opportunity.

AREA	CHALLENGE	HOW AI CAN HELP
Forecasting and pipeline management	■ Too many inaccurate forecasts ■ Limited pipeline visibility ■ Heavy administrative load on sales teams to keep systems updated	■ Predictive AI can analyze historical sales data and market trends to improve visibility into sales and pipeline forecasts to improve accuracy and focus team efforts. ■ Generative AI can help automate pipeline management tasks, providing real-time visibility into sales opportunities.
Sales and value management performance measurement	■ Difficulty in granular performance attribution ■ Suboptimal adoption of value automation tools and business cases	■ In advanced value management programs, both value management consultants and sellers are tasked with KPIs at an individual level. ■ Predictive AI can help forecast and measure relevant KPIs and metrics, whereas generative AI can automate performance tracking and analysis at a granular level.
Sales training and enablement	■ Training resource constraints ■ Inability to accommodate personalized training needs	■ AI solutions can help analyze the performance of sales reps and value engineers to help tailor training programs. ■ Generative AI can quickly create interactive training modules and simulations for on-demand learning based on learning preferences.
Engagement planning	It takes extensive report development and customization for: ■ Reporting on accounts, opportunities, and engagements ■ Performing analysis on accounts, opportunities, and engagements to identify which opportunities require business case development support or are currently at risk	■ AI chatbots designed for database Q&A can provide real-time answers to questions like "Which new deals require value management support?" and "Which deal needs urgent help?" ■ Given the dynamic nature of sales opportunities, AI assistants can bring much needed agility. ■ To retrieve useful results, AI assistants can be trained to understand standard queries, and translate and run SQL-type queries; they can also run code interpretation on CRM data to provide aggregate results from datasets.

Continues

Table 6.1 (*continued*)

AREA	CHALLENGE	HOW AI CAN HELP
Technology components for all of the preceding use cases:		

- Foundation models such as OpenAI and Google Gemini
- Database
- Application layer
- User interface
- APIs
- Custom AI development using assistants or agentic AI

Making the Business Case for Value Engineering Programs: The ROI of ROI Programs

A key responsibility for sales and value leaders is securing funding for value management programs. This requires forecasting the potential benefits of these ROI programs—specifically, their impact on pipeline expansion, revenue growth, renewals, and business expansion. An intriguing question for every value leader is: "How do you forecast the ROI of your ROI program?"

This analysis is often part of long-range planning, and this is where the sales operations team plays a critical role. They provide historical data, future forecasts, and a deep understanding of the systems—all of which are essential to building a solid business case.

Ironically, even highly successful value programs face scrutiny. As the team scales, budgets often come under pressure during times of slowed revenue growth. Overhead costs, including management layers, support resources, and platforms like ROI calculators, become prime targets for cost-cutting. Let's explore the cost components of a value management program (see Table 6.2).

Table 6.2: Investment Costs of Value Programs

COST COMPONENT	DESCRIPTION
Labor	The largest investment, primarily due to the experience and compensation needed for a strong business value services team. Team sizes range from a few to hundreds.

COST COMPONENT	DESCRIPTION
Digital Tools	SaaS platforms that automate business case development and scaling key processes.
Travel & Expenses	Necessary for executive briefings and events that help promote and communicate the business case.
Training & Adoption	Critical for scaling value programs across the entire enterprise sales team.
Content & Data Subscriptions	Costs include hiring vendors to create content, subscriptions for industry data, and expenses for client engagement (gifts, awards, etc.).

Key Outcomes of Value Programs

Let's now look at the tangible business outcomes that value programs drive:

- Expanded Pipelines: Business value consultants articulate possibilities early in the sales cycle, expanding existing pipelines and creating new ones. Their thought leadership and business acumen resonate with decision-makers, allowing even smaller vendors to engage large customers.

- Increased Revenue & Margins: Effective business value practices boost win rates, deal profitability, and overall revenue. By focusing on high-value deals and nurturing strategic partnerships, they increase deal sizes and overall margins.

- Reduced Churn & Upselling: Strengthening relationships with C-level executives and delivering on promised value reduces customer churn. Additionally, during renewals, a solid business case for further value helps upsell and expand the account.

Optimizing the ROI from ROI Programs

Here are a few ideas to consider:

- Focus on High-impact Deals: Prioritize complex solutions that have significant business impacts. Set thresholds to concentrate efforts on large, strategic deals.

- Robust Operating Model: Establish clear workflows, roles, and responsibilities to ensure value consultants are integrated into the sales cycle efficiently.

- Full Product & Solution Coverage: Develop value models across your entire portfolio to increase deal coverage and consistency.

- Address the Full Customer Lifecycle: Apply value management principles across sales, marketing, and customer success teams to improve lead generation and customer retention.

- Executive Buy-in: Gaining the commitment of sales leadership is essential for ensuring smooth collaboration between the value team and enterprise sales. Executive sponsorship is one of the most critical success factors in delivering positive ROI.

It's not just your customers who demand an ROI forecast for the product you are selling. Your management also needs to see the revenue impact of the value management program they are funding, or the ROI from doing the work!

Chapter 7, "Empowering Your Sales Partners with AI-Driven Value Management," discusses how value management practices can supercharge customer success programs and, when combined with AI solutions, can drive exponentially greater customer renewals and retention. It's a timely discussion because the convergence between value management and customer success has been a topic of intense debate and rapid evolution in recent years.

7

Empowering Your Sales Partners with AI-Driven Value Management

In the B2B economy, it's estimated that over 70 percent of a product's sales can come from revenue generated by partners.[1] That means it's absolutely essential for B2B enterprises to build a strong channel and partner sales capability. For industries ranging from healthcare and automotive to high tech and more, "ecosystem" partners are indispensable to B2B companies seeking to drive growth and profits. Simply put, partners provide essential business services and complementary products that help companies deliver what their customers are expecting: seamless integration with the customer's existing systems, faster and better business processes, widespread product adoption, and, above all, predictable business outcomes.

In this chapter we will group partners into two segments as follows:

- Tiered ecosystem: Partners are divided into categories based on size and skills.

- Partner types: Partners are segmented based on business roles and include resellers, system integrators (SIs), and technology alliance partners.

---

[1] "Channel partners to drive more than 70% of IT spending in 2023," ChannelFutures (https://www.channelfutures.com/channel-business/channel-partners-to-drive-more-than-70-of-it-spending-in-2023).

Many large enterprise product companies use a combination of these two groupings to organize their partner channel relationships.

Not surprisingly, partner sales channels can be huge, reflecting the significant resources partners expend on deploying products at complex enterprise-scale companies. Indeed, the size of the channel can dwarf that of the customers they serve. For manufacturing industries, the scale of partner channel sales is similar, with an estimate of 75 percent of total world trade conducted via indirect sales.[2]

The Risk of a Poor Partner Experience

Given the high stakes, B2B companies can face severe consequences if they poorly manage their partner's performance. As an extension of the B2B company's brand, the partner can easily damage their client's business, putting their reputation, revenue, and customer base at risk— perhaps even causing problems with employee hiring and retention. These risks are real because at the end of the day, the customer expects your products to perform flawlessly for their business. And as numerous CIOs, board members, and business leaders told us in researching this book, the onus of performance lies squarely on the company that built the product.

Bad experiences with a reselling or implementation partner are legion: a reseller that fails to deliver critical products to customer's factory, data center, or headquarters on time, delaying a crucial rollout; a system implementer that botches a big solution integration, breaking the project's budget; or an alliance partner whose key product doesn't work as promised, causing headaches for the customer for months. Regardless who's at fault, the company gets an earful and lives with the fallout for months to years to come.

In our 20-plus years in the technology industry, we can point to numerous examples of partners who were poorly managed by the tech provider, leading to disastrous results for the customer and vendor alike.

One recent example we witnessed involved a global telecom client that planned to invest in a popular enterprise CRM SaaS solution. After being presented with an upbeat business case prepared by the SaaS company, which projected solid revenue and productivity improvements, the telecom's board of directors greenlit the investment. Indeed,

---

[2] "The guide to channel sales for manufacturers," Freshworks (https://www.freshworks.com/crm/industries/manufacturing/channel-sales-guide).

the telecom was so convinced of the solution's benefits that they baked rosy expectations of revenue growth and cost savings into their financial forecast. All looked bright for the SaaS project! To lead the deployment, the SaaS company recommended a well-respected system integrator (SI) that brought both industry and product expertise and had successfully deployed other IT solutions for the telecom.

But the project ran into trouble right away. Although many of the problems couldn't be pinned on the SaaS vendor of its SI partner, the company's board wasn't looking for excuses and placed a close watch on the project, constantly pressing the SaaS vendor and SI on when the promised business results would start showing up. After two years of lackluster outcomes, the board had seen enough and pulled the plug on the project—or what the board called an "indefinite pause." The SI was abruptly shown the door, severely damaging its relationship with the telecom, while the SaaS provider lost its contract with the company. The debacle threatened to ruin the SaaS company's reputation in the telecom industry, as other telecoms learned of the company's stumble and started rethinking their SaaS investments. This is just one example of thousands of projects that have upended B2B companies looking to scale their solutions through ecosystem partners.

De-risking Partner Relationships

So, what can a B2B company do to avoid these pitfalls? The truth is, building and managing an effective sales channel and partner ecosystem can be extremely difficult, with partner communities that can encompass thousands of companies across the globe. Since each partner brings its own set of skills and business-value contributions to customers, managing them as one monolithic group is not reasonable.

Weighing how and when to bring partners into a deal, how to ensure coordination across partners, and monitoring their performance can be an overwhelming job for B2B companies. Yet successfully orchestrating the channel to engage customers is a crucial skill for companies to master if they expect to build market trust and translate successful product implementations into revenue growth.

Let's now dig deeper into the partner channel relationship, looking at each of the different partner ecosystem tiers, the different types of partners you'll find in each tier, and how AI can empower B2B enterprises to deliver one-to-one individualized attention to each partner in the ecosystem.

Partner Ecosystems Tiers

In the tiered ecosystem approach, introduced above, enterprises segment partners based on their various capabilities working with customers. The top tier includes companies that provide customers with high-level strategic consulting capabilities and includes global companies such as Accenture, Deloitte, and PwC. Middle-tier companies provide services that focus on driving operational improvements and may also bring specific regional experience, industry knowledge, or specialized technical expertise. The bottom tier can include companies with a mix of narrower capabilities, such as expertise in point solutions, highly specialized technical skills, or innovative solutions that are emerging and may serve unique market niches in the future.

Figure 7.1 illustrates a simple example of a partner ecosystem.

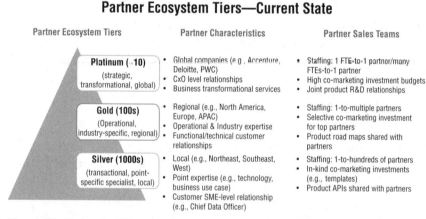

Partner Ecosystem Tiers—Current State

Partner Ecosystem Tiers	Partner Characteristics	Partner Sales Teams
Platinum (~10) (strategic, transformational, global)	• Global companies (e.g., Accenture, Deloitte, PWC) • CxO level relationships • Business transformational services	• Staffing: 1 FTE-to-1 partner/many FTEs-to-1 partner • High co-marketing investment budgets • Joint product R&D relationships
Gold (100s) (Operational, industry-specific, regional)	• Regional (e.g., North America, Europe, APAC) • Operational & Industry expertise • Functional/technical customer relationships	• Staffing: 1-to-multiple partners • Selective co-marketing investment for top partners • Product road maps shared with partners
Silver (1000s) (transactional, point-specific specialist, local)	• Local (e.g., Northeast, Southeast, West) • Point expertise (e.g., technology, business use case) • Customer SME-level relationship (e.g., Chief Data Officer)	• Staffing: 1-to-hundreds of partners • In-kind co-marketing investments (e.g., templates) • Product APIs shared with partners

Figure 7.1: Enterprise B2B company: partner ecosystem example

The typical ecosystem includes three to four tiers of partners, forming a pyramid with the most strategic, largest partners at the top and the smaller and more specialized companies at the bottom. The tiering allows the B2B companies to easily find partners that are form-fit to the types of services each tier provides.

The challenge for B2B companies is how to best deploy value management best practices across all these tiers. Let's look at how companies in each tier address typical challenges:

Top-tier partners attract large investments from B2B sponsors but suffer from poor engagement.   The largest partners typically secure significantly more resources from the B2B company, despite being only a small fraction of their channel. The company's sales teams may struggle to promote value management approaches with partners because of the fragmented nature of the partner's sales organization, which can maintain dozens of teams split between consulting solutions, industries, and clients. They also can struggle to get the attention of the partner's executives because of differences over who owns the customer relationship. One example is the time we worked with a Fortune 500 retailer that used a global SI for their merchandising modernization program. The SI partner claimed ownership of the relationship with the retailer's most important decision-makers (the CIO and the VP of merchandising), leaving the product company to settle for secondhand reports from the customer's IT staff or by nagging the SI partner for updates. Bottom line: The SI considered the product company simply a vendor instead of a strategic partner.

Middle-tier partners, with smaller deal sizes, struggle to find ways to grow.   Middle-tier partners drive a greater number of sales, but each deal is smaller on average than their top-tier peers. But these mid-range partners can still be quite large, with revenues reaching in the hundreds of millions of dollars per year. Oracle, for example, relies on hundreds of mid-tier partners to implement the company's financial management and cloud solutions and contribute unique geographic, industry, or technical experience. Many of these partners also serve large-scale customers, such as government agencies, top auto suppliers, and Fortune 2000 companies—and some are gunning to join the top tier by proving that their expertise matches that of their top competitors. Our work with many of these mid-tier partners has found that they often have a love–hate relationship with their product company sponsors. The partners believe that if their OEMs invested more in joint go-to-market programs, they would accelerate revenue growth and gain share. Often, we have been left with the question of how this tier could be more efficiently managed to generate better results.

Bottom-tier partners' specialization helps outperform, but targeted investments can drive more growth.   Sometimes, the smallest partners can garner outsized gains with niche solutions and services that drive substantial value for major-league customers. For example, we worked with a partner that helps design solutions for hospital operating rooms that has gained the trust of some of the world's biggest healthcare companies. The partner provides system-configuration expertise that certifies the product will meet the most stringent requirements of a hospital operating room. Its specialized expertise gives the hospital confidence that the vendor's product will perform in a demanding medical environment. Although this partner occupies the lower tier in size, it is probably one of the most strategic and best-performing partners across any of the tiers. To better serve these partners in this lower tier, the sponsoring company needs to devise business value–based sales and marketing programs that feed the partner's sales funnel and support growth without adding new bureaucratic processes that can distract the partners from their work with the customer.

AI-Enabled Partner-Based Value Management (AI-PBVM)

Creating and managing a successful partner channel is a daunting task for many B2B companies. That's why we're excited about a new AI-driven value management approach that can streamline and optimize partner programs and unlock greater potential for ecosystems. With this new approach, enabled by AI, B2B companies leverage the same account-based marketing (ABM) techniques we explored in Chapter 4, "AI-Driven Value Management for Marketing," but apply those principles to running their partner ecosystems. We're calling this new approach *AI-enabled partner-based value management*, or AI-PBVM.

VM PRO TIP

As AI enables partner marketing teams to scale its support of the partner channel, adopting a similar approach to how marketing uses ABM to engage customers will be a game changer for the channel. Now partners will be able to augment their value management capabilities and engage in a coordinated, fully customized value conversation with their customers. This will greatly enhance the channel sales results for small to medium-sized customers for the sponsor company.

This new approach aims to empower both sides of the partner relationship with one-to-one (e.g., personalized) go-to-market capabilities augmented by AI tools. It works like this: The company's partner sales team works with an AI-generated *digital twin* that is specifically trained to support their partner's value management programs. A digital twin is a virtual representation of a physical object, system, or process. When properly trained, the digital twin can understand the partner's strengths and limitations and continually learn from ongoing customer projects.

Based on output from the digital twin, companies can recommend the right partner for each deal and even decide to not bring certain partners into a deal. What that means is a dramatic change in the nature of the relationship at each tier.

WINNING WITH TWINS

Generative AI and digital twins can radically improve how B2B companies and their ecosystem partners go to market by helping rapidly create joint marketing programs informed by each other's value propositions.

AI-powered digital twins will help partners cost-effectively scale their marketing resources. For example, the partner's marketing team could train the digital twin to "understand" their products' value propositions and then ask it to combine that content with the OEM's solutions, enabling the team to quickly develop a joint value proposition and go-to-market approach.

The AI twin could also provide recommendations and autogenerate co-branded content that communicates the shared value proposition of the two companies.

We believe the adoption of AI-enabled partner programs will drive broader use of value management practices and multiply desired business outcomes across all the partner tiers (see Figure 7.2). These outcomes include:

- Tight alignment across the customer life cycle
- Rapid production of one-to-one co-branded marketing assets with quantified business value
- Streamlined orchestration of joint value-selling motions across multiple channels, both digital and in-person
- Co-managed customer success activities, including quarterly business reviews (QBRs), meetings, and joint reference activities
- Continuous learning and joint-solution improvement opportunities

To drive integration between OEMs and their partner ecosystems, companies will rely on generative AI's native ability to find and synthesize data from multiple sources, much of it previously locked away in information "silos" within each organization. Indeed, many of the business leaders we talked to called out AI's critical role in extracting key insights across data repositories and doing so in near real time at less cost.

Partner Ecosystem Tiers—PBM Relationship

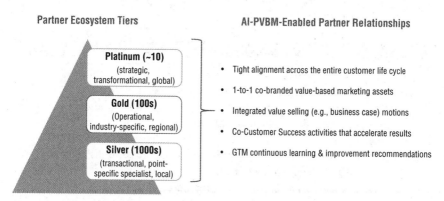

Figure 7.2: AI-enabled partner-based value management (AI-PBVM)

"One of the largest opportunities for AI will be to aggregate previously independent sources of information," said Bob Lim, who has over 20 years of C-suite experience and is currently VP of information technology and CIO of San Jose State University. "There are many opportunities across our landscape to bring dispersed datasets together to provide rapid and simplified access to questions that may take multiple searches and aggregation today."

Top Tier—AI-PBVM Unifies Go-to-Market Activities

Many top-tier partners are already practicing one-to-one AI-enabled partner-based value management (AI-PBVM) approaches and reaping tangible business benefits. By enhancing joint sales and marketing programs with value-based evidence enhanced by data from an AI digital twin, the two partners can significantly strengthen and unify their go-to-market motions (see Table 7.1). For example, partners can more quickly uncover industry insights and quantify product and project performance, helping produce more relevant, value-based marketing content for prospects. Similarly, output from the AI digital twins can help sales teams share relevant value messaging and insights about the customer, such as industry value drivers, business use cases, and customer reference assets—all designed to help the teams build an optimal sales proposal for the client.

Table 7.1: Top-tier AI-PBVM use cases

#	ACTIVITY	SOURCE	AI-ASSISTED ACTIONS
1	Co-marketing Digital Coordinator	Customer/Partner: Product systems, marketing platforms, value engineering systems, customer success systems, third-party industry research sources	The top-tier partners have large content management systems that include value management content, including industry benchmarks, customer references, and solution thought leadership that can be better used in joint-sales opportunities. The digital coordinator will autogenerate co-branded marketing assets for the top-tier partners that speak to the joint-value proposition. The AI marketing assistant will learn from past customer engagements and proposals to recommend the overall value proposition that speaks to specific customer segment needs (e.g., industry, region, size) and keep the messaging in step with new product and customer developments.
2	Co-Sales Partner Digital Value Consultant	Customer/Partner: Product systems, third-party research systems, value engineering systems, customer success systems	Leveraging the vast content resources of the partner and the product company, the co-sales partner sales digital value consultant will provide specific recommendations on how to custom-fit a solution's value proposition to the unique attributes of a customer deal. The digital assistant will help to coordinate between the top-tier partner account teams and the product sales team to optimize future sales funnel activities. The digital consultant will look not only at the product company's capabilities but also at the value that the partner provides to drive additional business impact and how a combination of partners can optimize the fit for that specific opportunity.

Continues

Table 7.1 (*continued*)

#	ACTIVITY	SOURCE	AI-ASSISTED ACTIONS
3	Co-Customer Success Digital Value Consultant	CRM systems, Value engineering systems, product systems, customer success systems, customer project folders	Top-tier partners will create enormous volumes of project materials, including project status updates, management review presentations, and ongoing business impact reports. The co-customer success digital value consultant will summarize all these materials with product telemetry data, customer success data, and the up-front business outcome targets from the value engineering systems to autogenerate a business outcomes realization report and a set of recommendations on future steps the customer can take to drive further business value.

Post-sales relationships between partners and their OEM sponsor will almost certainly improve. For example, AI-equipped "digital customer success consultants" will be able to closely track the business impact of products before and after the implementation and spanning multiple rollout phases. The two partners can now present a unified front to the customer, leveraging a customer value report autogenerated by the digital customer success consultant.

Middle Tier—AI-PBVM Automates Value Management Go-to-Market Messaging and Assets

Partners in the middle tier are ripe for AI-PBVM reinvention. Often underappreciated by their larger OEM sponsors, mid-market partners are held back by their limited marketing budgets and labor. This makes it hard for them to underwrite time-consuming and costly marketing programs and everything they entail, such as creating co-branded messaging, sponsoring customer events, and building a portfolio of go-to-market assets. This is where AI tools step in by cost-effectively augmenting the resources that OEMs had allocated to the middle tier and energizing this relationship in the process.

Using AI digital twins, the OEM's partner-focused marketers can now do more with less. A co-marketing digital twin will "learn" from the partner's sales presentations, engagement materials, and reference stories, and develop a joint value proposition that aligns the capabilities and products of both partners. The twin will autogenerate joint go-to-market content—such as co-branded brochures, infographics, videos, and whitepapers—and assist in igniting demand and promoting the partnership's unique value proposition to the marketplace. From a sales and customer success perspective, many of the same benefits that accrue to top-tier partners will apply to the mid-tier partners, including tighter sales and customer success coordination.

Table 7.2 describes a couple ways that AI-PBVM can help OEMs improve the business outcomes of their mid-tier partners.

Table 7.2:   Mid-tier AI-PBVM use cases

#	ACTIVITY	SOURCE	AI-ASSISTED ACTIONS
1	Co-marketing Digital Programs Management Twin	Customer/Partner: Product systems, marketing platforms, value engineering systems, customer success systems, third-party industry research sources	The digital twin plays a critical role in scaling this tier's small team of marketing and sales resources at their disposal. The digital twin will autogenerate co-branded marketing assets for the mid-tier partners, which speaks to the joint-value proposition of the two companies. The digital twin will help to scale and coordinate go-to-market activities of the partner and product company by assisting with operational activities such as generating content for events or supporting the creation of content for partner executives presenting at the sponsor's conference. The digital twin can also play a reporting role, analyzing results of past marketing campaigns to present results to leadership and recommend future actions to improve results.
2	Co-Sales Partner Digital Value Consultant	Customer/Partner: Product systems, third-party research systems, value engineering systems, customer success systems	The co-sales partner digital value consultant will provide specific recommendations on how to custom-fit a solution's value proposition to the unique attributes of a customer deal. The digital assistant will help to coordinate between the mid-tier partner sales teams and the product sales team to optimize future sales funnel activities. The digital consultant will look not only at the product company's capabilities but also at the value that the partner provides to drive additional business impact and how a combination of partners can optimize the fit for that specific opportunity.

Lower Tier—AI-PBVM Provides Virtual CMO and Value Engineering Resources

Smaller, more specialized partners will need to take a different approach to AI-PBVM programs. Most bottom-tier partners won't have access to the resources needed to fund go-to-market activities on the level of their upper-tier partners. In many cases, the partner's owners also serve as marketers, salespeople, and customer success managers for their organizations. The hospital operating room services company we talked about earlier fields a sales, marketing, and customer success team of one—the CEO. The rest of the company is made up of technical engineers who build and test the operating room systems.

For smaller partners, a turnkey partnership with their OEM sponsors is a necessity. An effective AI-PBVM program may include a "digital partner sales assistant" that plays a virtual consultative role—almost like a part-time chief marketing officer or chief revenue officer. The partner would rely on the digital assistant to create co-branded sales brochures and blogs, and even draft business cases. They could use the assistant to recommend the best industry events to attend or sponsor, decide what upcoming sales programs to participate in, and create customer reference content and industry KPIs.

It's often tough for smaller partners to gain visibility into their larger B2B sponsors and sales teams, which can act as a barrier to reaching new customers. Similarly, the larger OEM may be unaware of the partner's unique know-how or specialized services and thus fail to position them effectively to customers. The digital assistant can act as a bullhorn for the partner sales teams, automatically reaching out to the OEM whenever it runs into a new sales opportunity that matches the partner's skills and competitive strengths. One way the digital assistant can do that is by parsing through the sponsoring company's CRM system and flagging promising opportunities that are well suited for the partner (see Table 7.3).

Table 7.3:   Lower-tier AI-PBVM use cases

#	ACTIVITY	SOURCE	AI-ASSISTED ACTIONS
1	Co-marketing Digital Strategy & Program Twins	Customer/ Partner: Product systems, marketing platforms, value engineering systems, customer success systems, third-party industry research sources	Digital twins will help lower-tier partners develop a value-based marketing strategy, playing a fractional CMO role for the partner's leadership team. It will also autogenerate co-branded marketing assets for these partners, which help create a value-oriented joint-value proposition. The digital twin will help to scale go-to-market activities of the partner and product company by assisting with operational activities such as generating content for events or supporting the creation of content for partner executives presenting at the sponsor's conference.
2	Co-Sales Partner Digital Value Consultant	Customer/ Partner: Product systems, third-party research systems, value engineering systems, customer success systems	The co-sales partner sales digital value consultant will play the role of a part-time (or fractional) value engineer, providing value modeling recommendations for the partner's solutions. The digital value consultant will also help coordinate between the lower-tier leadership and the sponsor's sales team to optimize future sales funnel activities. The digital value consultant will match the partner's capabilities with sales opportunities that provide the right fit for a lower-tier partner.

Value Management for Three Types of Ecosystem Partners

For most B2B companies, the sales channel ecosystem is made up of three types of partners: system integrators, value-added resellers, and technology alliance partners. Each of these groups (see Figure 7.3) provides a useful "scaling mechanism" for enterprise-scale B2B product companies. In this section, we'll detail how AI can provide new avenues for growth across each of the partner categories. We'll explore how companies can leverage the technology to more quickly react to market shifts, empower the channel to sell more effectively, and scale existing partner teams to better support channel operations.

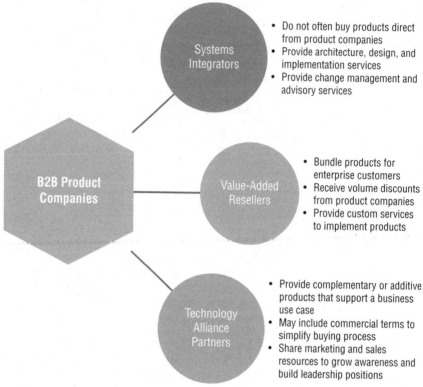

Figure 7.3: Partner channel categories

System Integrators: An Indispensable Partner

The global IT system integrator market is huge and getting bigger. It totaled about $430 billion in 2023 and is expected to grow about 9.9 percent a year through 2032.[3] For many B2B product companies, achieving global scale and maintaining market leadership would hardly be possible without a thriving partner channel. With their enormous scale and industry experience, SI companies like Accenture, Deloitte, Infosys, and IBM frequently serve as important strategic advisers to the vendor, helping map out how the tech provider's solution will fit into the customer's complex

---

[3] Market.US, "Global Systems Integration Market Report" (https://market.us/report/system-integration-services-market).

business and technical environments. The SI's goal is to successfully integrate the solution into the customer's existing technical architecture and business workflows and overcome any change-management obstacles.

Let's look at how IT buyers work with SIs and partners in the high-tech industry. Buyers typically start by looking for technology solutions that can help them reach their strategic goals. They may land on a single vendor or choose from a shortlist of competitive products. If there's a "bakeoff," the corporate planning team will make their vendor selection and move on to a more detailed planning stage.

This is when the buyer—even before the deal is closed—will reach out to a reputable system integrator and work with their consulting team to help define the scope of the project, draft an implementation plan, and determine budget requirements. Meanwhile, the vendor provides its licensing requirements and technical resources.

The SI team largely navigates the overall timeline, budget, and resources for the buyer with guidance from the buyer's technical team. Once the buyer has secured funding, the vendor may take a back seat to the proceedings and allow the SI to lead the implementation. The product company may occasionally participate in project status meetings and re-engage when the product is up for renewal (assuming it's an SaaS solution) or is reaching the end of its life cycle.

But it's a mistake for B2B companies to let down their guard. Implementations can often go awry, and the vendor may not notice it before it's too late. AI can help vendors stay on top of their SI's implementation project—and beyond. Fast action to get projects back on track can lead to better business outcomes and higher customer retention rates.

Today, we see three main use cases where AI tools can help improve SI and partner projects:

- Automating strategy-to-planning efforts for customer engagements
- Quickly creating proof-of-concepts that give prospective customers more confidence in a successful business outcome
- Providing accurate, customer-specific recommendations throughout the life cycle of an implementation project

LEANING ON SIs AND TECH PARTNERS TO HELP JUSTIFY MAJOR INVESTMENTS

Before spending millions of dollars on new technologies, smart buyers often seek the advice of top system integrators and tech partners. That's been standard practice for Ginna Raahauge, who for nearly three decades served as CIO and chief technology officer (CTOs) at several Fortune 100 companies, including the country's largest Catholic hospital chain.

"Having an SI…that can partner with my team to understand our business operating environment and IT landscape was critical to developing a great business case and gaining approval from my leadership team for major technology investments," Raahauge says. However, it wasn't easy for her to find an experienced partner that could deliver a sound business case in a timely manner. "I found only a handful of SIs and [tech partners] that truly had the resources to deliver what I felt was a convincing business case for the solutions we needed," she shares. "This meant I either needed to hire another consulting team to develop the business case, or my own team had to spend their scarce bandwidth on building a business case that would resonate with my leadership team."

Looking ahead, Raahauge—who is currently general manager and Field CTO for St. Louis–based World Wide Technology Inc. (WWT)—believes that more and more CIOs will lean on their SIs and tech partners to help justify their investments—and increasingly to deliver on the outcomes being promised. "Not only do I believe that a solid business case will be a requirement to gain budget for enterprise-level IT projects, but CIOs and CFOs will demand that these large projects deliver on the expectations set at the time of the investment," she says. "This will continue to raise the bar on value management discipline for SIs and tech vendors."

Automating Strategy-to-Planning Efforts with AI

One of the top priorities for B2B companies and their SI partners is convincing their shared customer prospects that investing in a multimillion-dollar solution makes sense. These conversations can take months to play out and involve a whirlwind of activities and meetings that can include:

- Multiday trips to the B2B company's executive briefing center
- Multiple onsite customer workshops to gain buy-in from both client technical and business teams
- A series of internal planning sessions between the SI and the vendor's account teams
- Creating dozens of strategic presentations, business cases, implementation plans, and detailed budget schedules

As you can imagine, the resources and time required from everybody—the buyer, the SI, and the vendor's product teams—can be overwhelming.

"One of the biggest challenges for vendors and systems integrators alike is the time commitment they place on their buyers to build a business case," says Patty Morrison, a veteran business executive who worked as CIO at Office Depot, Motorola, and Cardinal Health and currently serves on the board of directors of healthcare giant Baxter International.

In our interview for this book, Morrison recalled the time when her company was looking to invest in a large-scale SAP software solution. "[The vendor] would ask our leadership team to go offsite at their executive briefing center for 6 weeks to customize the business case and build the implementation plan for our company," she says. "GenAI solutions will play a big role in helping reduce the effort that these companies will demand of their customers in the future."

Using AI solutions trained in technology project implementations, SIs and product vendors can transform how they support their customers from start to finish, accelerating implementation timelines and reducing costs dramatically. For example, instead of taking weeks to months to build an implementation plan for a big SaaS project, an AI planning assistant could help vendors and their SI partners complete the task in days and at a fraction of the cost. The AI assistant does this by:

- Rapidly ingesting key data and generating a profile of the customer's strategic priorities

- Identifying key business KPIs that the vendor's solution can improve, helping generate a solid business case

- Integrate these insights with past implementation data to draft an accurate project plan

We've already seen early versions of the AI-driven process that is driving productivity improvements at several of our clients. For example, one SI created an Oracle project-scoping tool that takes key data and variables from a prospective customer and automatically drafts a preliminary project plan and budget in just three days compared to what used to be a three-month process.

Morrison suggests that CIOs and other top customer executives should meet with product vendors at the start of every project, allowing the vendor to collect key data points—including the customer's existing IT architecture, their various business processes, and key cost variables—and then draft a "current state" view of the prospect's operating environment. From this initial meeting, the GenAI planning tool takes over, quickly generating a set of strategic recommendations, a detailed business case, and an initial implementation plan. This enables executives on the buyer's side to rapidly determine whether the vendor meets their business needs and move forward with the implementation/investment.

No longer burdened by up-front data analysis and planning work, the vendor and SI teams can focus on reviewing and validating the AI-generated plans and refining them based on their on-the-ground expertise and interactions with the customer.

Accelerating Proofs-of-Concept for Faster Customer Buy-in

Large investment projects almost always come with financial and operational risk. Anyone who's implemented large enterprise resource planning (ERP) projects or installed new technologies in a factory has heard the horror stories of a multimillion-dollar implementation gone wrong. Proofs-of-concept (PoCs) are a great way to make sure a company doesn't make such a big mistake, convincing management that they're likely to realize the business outcomes promised by the vendor and SI. But PoCs themselves can be expensive to design and execute, tying up resources from all the players—buyers, vendors, and SIs.

Planning the PoC can be a time- and resource-intensive effort, as teams work to identify and design a small subset of the full solution—often referred to as a minimally viable product (MVP)—to be deployed as a stand-alone prototype showing what the final product could do for the company. However, teams often struggle to line up the mix of resources needed from the customer, SI, and vendor teams, which can delay the launch of the PoC and potentially throw the sales process offtrack.

And as you are learning by now, this is where AI tools can streamline and accelerate the whole process. In the same way that aerospace and auto manufacturers speed time-to-market with the help of product simulators, what if AI could help create a PoC simulator? Today it's possible. Imagine an AI simulator that ingests the customer's technical and business profile, creating a *digital twin* of the customer that simulates how the product would work in real life.

AI-generated digital twins could sidestep a host of manual tasks associated with PoCs, including:

- Access and integration to customer systems
- System configuration

- User testing and results reporting
- Coordinating resource availability—PoC client, SI, and independent software vendor (ISV)/OEM experts

Thus, AI-driven digital twins would provide the same advantages of simulators found in other industries, including lower costs, increased speed to test results, and greater flexibility to adjust the approach based on PoC results.

Providing Accurate Implementation Recommendations

For anybody who's worked on large enterprise technology projects, you know one thing is certain: Your best-laid plans will change during the course of the implementation. Success depends on project leaders who can spot emerging problems and quickly adjust plans, resources, and strategies accordingly.

Drawing from past experiences, project managers and executives help SIs avert costly missteps and keep implementations on schedule and on budget. As shown in Table 7.4, AI tools will offer SIs a flexible new resource to help identify potential issues and recommend smart solutions quickly. Imagine an AI platform that ingests plans from every previous project using the same technology; combs through team communications dealing with similar problems and the mitigation tactics used; analyzes the results of those actions; and then combines all these insights into a set of recommendations in minutes to help SIs confidently steer the project forward.

Humans will still play a role in B2B technology (and other) implementations. AI models will need proper oversight by SI partners and the technology providers to ensure that an AI "recommendation engine" is accurately interpreting past projects. And experienced human managers will still need to be on hand to ensure the AI-driven recommendations properly address the project's changing requirements. But if an AI recommendations engine can provide even basic guidance, such as providing timely, accurate advice to junior project managers or streamlining research into project options, then the investment would be well worth it.

Table 7.4: System implementers (SIs) value management digital tools

#	ACTIVITY	SOURCE	AI-ASSISTED ACTIONS
1	AI Strategy to Planning Automation Recommendations Engine	Customer/ Partner: Product systems, marketing platforms, value engineering systems, customer success systems, third-party industry research sources	The AI strategy-to-planning recommendation engine will streamline a critical step in the effort to close large enterprise projects. By using an AI strategic planning toolset, deal teams will be able to leverage the learning capabilities of AI to capture customer data and build a strategic plan that outlines the strategic, financial, and operational impact of the SI and OEM's solution. Instead of needing to collect data from customer interviews, public financial sources, and researching past customer engagement materials, the AI tool will comb these sources to deliver a data-rich report for the deal team.
2	AI Proof-of-Concept Acceleration Toolset	Customer/ Partner: Product systems, third-party research systems, value engineering systems, customer success systems	The AI PoC Acceleration toolset will ingest the customer's profile and the scope of the proposed solution, then match it against prior customer experiences to rapidly stand up a solution pilot for the customer.
3	AI Implementation Recommendation Engine	Customer/ Partner: Product systems, CRM, value engineering systems, customer success systems	The AI implementation recommendation engine will play a critical role in designing future customer implementation plans. Leveraging the insights across hundreds of deployment teams, the AI toolset will develop best-fit implementation models for new projects.

HOW AN ORACLE PARTNER SI'S VALUE MANAGEMENT STRATEGY PAID OFF

Partners of some of the world's largest B2B companies are boosting sales by adopting value management strategies. We found a powerful example in a mid-sized SI that specializes in helping its enterprise clients implement cloud-based business applications from Oracle, one of the world's largest technology providers.

Like many of Oracle's mid-tier partners, this company is run by a small group of executives led by its founder, who serves as its president, brand champion, and team cheerleader. On any given day, you'll find him rallying his sales team, managing customer relationships, and hiring and inspiring his workforce.

Going up against industry titans like Deloitte and Accenture can be intimidating for smaller SIs, but when a big sales opportunity emerged at a leading global shipping provider, this Oracle partner tried a new tactic: showing the business value his organization had recently delivered to a company in a closely related industry. In other words, the partner adopted a value management approach to the deal, backed by business value messaging and results tailored to the potential customer—not just features and functions.

Sure enough, the value-based pitch—combined with the presence of its A-team leaders—quickly turned the tide of the deal and delivered a win for the partner, which beat out its much larger rivals.

Rolling Out Value Management

The success of this value management strategy made a big impression on the partner's founder, who promptly asked us to help his small executive team bolster the approach and create effective value messaging for its customers going forward. We started by putting together three key value-based marketing and sales initiatives:

- **Event marketing:** We worked with the partner to uplift and scale the messaging it presents at Oracle's big annual conference—Oracle CloudWorld—and at smaller, regional events.

- **Digital marketing:** Because the partner had little brand recognition outside of Oracle, we helped it create cost-effective digital marketing campaigns built around its success at producing business value for customers, helping the partner stand out in a crowded marketplace.

- **Value engineering tool:** One of the keys to the partner's ability to outcompete the big SIs was a detailed ROI model created by the company's sales director, which forecasted an individualized business value profile for each prospective customer of using the company's cloud-migration service offering. We helped convert the value model into a popular sales tool that salespeople use today to accelerate new deals. The model also formed the basis of a successful lead-generation tool to attract more prospects.

Program Results

As expected, these value management initiatives generated measurable improvements in the sales funnel in just a few months, as shown here.

Bias—Partner caselet results

CAMPAIGN RESULTS THROUGH 6 MONTHS

Google Ads   Linked in ads

7,000   300+
clicks   form fills from ads

Email Phase 1
24,500 EMAILS SENT -2 AUDIENCES

Email Phase 2
SENT TO LEAD SCORE 40+

4.9% 2.6%   31%
avg. open rate   click thru rate   avg. open rate

Results: 350+ net new leads in first 6 months

The founder was ecstatic when he discovered that his decision to embrace value management worked as intended, and over the following months the company steadily incorporated *value intelligence* into the core messages on its website, social media channels, and go-to-market sales presentations and tools. The partner's name became more visible across the Oracle partner community, elevating it to premium brand status. Shortly thereafter, the founder was approached by a top global consulting firm and was acquired at a price the founder called "too good to pass up."

Value-Added Resellers—A Critical Link in the Value Chain

Many of the largest B2B industries also benefit from a robust value-added reseller (VAR) channel capability. This partner cohort helps customers source, aggregate, and implement B2B products across a variety of products. For example, a CIO looking to source products for their company's data center may use a VAR to aggregate the purchasing of servers, storage, networking gear, power supplies, and more. VARs help companies procure the products, implement them, and then maintain them throughout their life cycle.

For tech vendors, VARs play an important role in extending their market coverage to large customers that use their products as part of a larger solution. Think of NVIDIA and Intel, whose chips are essential components of larger computer systems used across a myriad of industries and applications. These reselling partners help reduce the original manufacturer's sales costs by optimizing logistics and distribution operations and ensuring the tech manufacturers' products are configured correctly for customers.

VALUE-ADDED RESELLER WITH A VALUE MANAGEMENT MINDSET

St. Louis–based Worldwide Technology (WWT) is a good example of a VAR in the high-tech industry. WWT helps leading tech companies such as NVIDIA, Cisco, HPE, and Intel sell and distribute their products globally. Today, WWT has over $20 billion in revenue, employing over 10,000 people. Supporting its manufacturing partners, WWT's success has been driven by its focus on its customers, delivering solution engineering expertise combined with OEM product distribution to deliver projects on time and on budget with proven results.

B2B tech providers often help resellers offset their costs by funding co-marketing programs such as customer events, trade shows, and co-branded go-to-market content. But despite these programs, the two partners often keep an arms-length relationship, making it tough for tech providers to bring their VARs up to speed on value-based messaging and how it can drive more deals with their common end customers. This is yet another opportunity for AI to shine. Here are two areas we believe AI-driven value management solutions can supercharge the relationship between B2B companies and their VARs, fueling sales growth.

AI-Powered Co-marketing Assistant

AI tools trained on value management content can be turned into a virtual marketing assistant for VARs that automatically generates value management–infused sales and marketing messages. The AI output would combine the VAR's unique capabilities with those of the original manufacturer, forming the basis for marketing assets such as value calculators and maturity assessment tools and joint customer success stories, and help identify new top-of-funnel prospects that can mutually benefit the two companies.

Digital Sales Consultant for VARs

With the help of industry-focused AI-VM tools, sales teams at VARs can ask (and get answers to) a range of questions to better position the manufacturers' products in front of customers. Such digital value management consultants would analyze past implementations and show the value realized by end customers thanks to the channel partnership. Industry use cases and benchmarks, rapidly produced by the AI tool, will paint a full picture of the business value opportunity for customers. Table 7.5 shows some examples of how AI-VM tools can help improve business outcomes for VARs.

Table 7.5: VAR AI digital assistant use cases

#	ACTIVITY	SOURCE	AI-ASSISTED ACTIONS
1	VAR Co-Marketing Value Management Assistant	Customer/Partner: Product systems, marketing platforms, value engineering systems, customer success systems, third-party industry research sources	Autogenerate co-branded marketing assets that speak to the joint-value proposition of the VAR and the product company. The AI marketing assistant will learn from customer engagements and proposals to recommend the overall VAR/OEM value proposition that speaks to specific customer segment needs, such as industry, region, or size.

#	ACTIVITY	SOURCE	AI-ASSISTED ACTIONS
2	Co-Sales VAR Digital Value Consultant	Customer/ Partner: Product systems, third-party research systems, value engineering systems, customer success systems	The co-sales VAR digital value consultant will provide specific recommendations on how to custom-fit a solution's value proposition to the unique attributes of a customer deal. The digital assistant will help coordinate between the OEM sales teams and the VAR sales team to optimize sales funnel activities. The digital consultant will not only look at the product company's capabilities but also the value that the VAR provides to drive additional business impact, helping to quantify and develop business outcome KPIs and create business cases for each deal.

Technology Alliance Partners

Many enterprise-level B2B companies have successfully grown their business with the help of partners that sell complementary products or services. These "technology alliance partners" work together with their larger ally to solve one or more aspects of their customer's business problem. In the technology industry, there are many examples of these symbiotic relationships. Take the partnership between Cisco and Nuance. Nuance, a leading maker of contact center software provides Cisco a voice-to-text intelligence solution that integrates with the Cisco product, thereby providing a better call center experience for Cisco customers.

Although we are convinced that similar technology alliances can be strengthened with the help of value management programs, too often we see alliances languish due to the lack of funding and limited access to resources. Even the best-run programs face shortages of people and funding needed to support productive collaborations and keep partnerships in sync.

Add AI into the mix and the outlook changes, as alliance partners free up resources by automating many labor-intensive tasks, from content and message creation to partner communications. Technology partners benefit by enabling:

- Faster updating of product innovations
- Better coordination of resources, driving sales by enabling the partners to show a "unified front"
- More consistent and timely customer success activities to ensure renewals and reduce churn

Let's look at a few use cases where AI can boost alliance partnerships.

AI-Enabled Alliance Assistants

It can be hard for alliance managers to keep up with their principal partners' fast-moving technical and market innovations, which can result in a misalignment of their go-to-market efforts. The gap can be filled by AI tools we call "alliance assistants." These AI-powered tools can help alliance managers regularly check in with their lead partners to keep track of their evolving product plans and suggest ways that recent or upcoming changes might fit into the alliance partner's own product plans. Alliance managers can now better coordinate with their contacts in the larger company while leveraging value-focused market messaging to enhance go-to-market initiatives at scale.

AI Sales Consultant

It's not uncommon for large B2B technology providers to have hundreds of sales reps, compared to their smaller tech partners, who might scrape by with just a handful of alliance managers. That makes it nearly impossible for the alliance partner to get the attention of the lead company's sales teams and to effectively communicate the business value of its complementary (or embedded) solutions.

Now imagine another AI tool—we'll call it an "AI deal consultant"—that sales reps would interact with to gain fast insights into how a given alliance partner could accelerate a sales deal with solutions that complement and add value to the company's current or proposed products. Insights generated by the virtual consultant could include guidance on industry-specific use cases and how the two company's combined solutions would help meet industry requirements. With an AI deal consultant by its side, the account team can quickly build a well-articulated, joint ROI business case without calling on the overworked and understaffed technology alliance team.

AI Value Assistants for Renewals

Today, as more and more products are being sold as subscriptions that need to be renewed regularly, technology alliance partners no longer have the luxury of "one and done" sales transactions. Increasingly, they are under pressure to track renewal cycles and mobilize resources to make sure customers continue their subscription plan.

Renewal events are not always automatic. Customers today are more sophisticated in their budgeting processes and often demand proof that subscription products are delivering meaningful results before renewing their contracts. Unfortunately, alliance partners rarely have the bandwidth to take on new responsibilities like renewal management. Increasingly, they will need to find ways to automate and scale these tasks. (See Chapter 8, "AI-Driven Value Management for Customer Success," for more insight into this new go-to-market capability.)

Once more, AI can fill the gap, empowering alliance partners to stay on top of retention risks and delivering relevant insights and assets to close renewal deals. AI assistants can comb through reams of existing documents in minutes, including customer business cases and project status reports, and dig into customer records to understand user adoption performance. All these will give alliance managers what they need to support the renewal sales process with business value results aimed at securing future revenue streams (see Table 7.6).

Table 7.6:   Technology alliance partner AI digital assistant use cases

#	ACTIVITY	SOURCE	AI-ASSISTED ACTIONS
1	AI-enabled Alliance Assistants	Technology alliance partner and OEM product systems, third-party research content, marketing content systems	The innovation assistant will help to identify industry use cases that are supported by joint alliance partner and product company solutions. The assistant will define and capture industry KPIs and support the ability for the two companies to create go-to-market marketing and sales value tools (e.g., lead-gen tools, sales ROI calculators, and value realization dashboards). The assistant will also play a coordination role, keeping up with new generations of solutions to ensure alignment across companies. The assistant will recommend updates to the go-to-market value messaging and tools to keep up with future product innovation.

Continues

Table 7.6: (*continued*)

#	ACTIVITY	SOURCE	AI-ASSISTED ACTIONS
2	AI Deal Consultant	Customer/Partner: Product systems, marketing platforms, value engineering platforms, customer success systems, third-party industry research sources	The digital innovation assistant will provide joint solution insights to the alliance partner sales and product sales teams. The assistant will become an expert in the synergies between the two companies' solutions. The assistant will identify customer use cases and help the sales teams measure the impact of these solutions to accelerate and win more deals.
3.	AI Value Assistants for Renewals	Customer/Partner: Product systems, value engineering platforms, customer success systems	AI value assistants for renewals will help the product and alliance sales teams better communicate the combined business impact of their solutions. The assistant will review product data, business cases, customer presentations, value engineering tools, and customer success data to determine the current value realized by a customer and present opportunities to expand the business impact through the deployment of complementary products and services to gain greater share-of-wallet.

Conclusion

Partner channels are essential to the growth and profitability of B2B companies, frequently generating the lion's share of product revenue. AI partner-based value management (AI-PBVM) programs offer a new platform for companies to rethink go-to-market activities across the tiers and types of partnerships they maintain today. Well-positioned AI digital assistants and virtual consultants will provide a one-to-one partnership capability not available today.

New AI-driven value management solutions designed for partners will give B2B companies the power to deliver one-to-one individualized attention to its ecosystem partners. The result will be greater consistency in messaging and greater depth in value intelligence. And by integrating the unique capabilities and talents of both partners, the AI platform will help companies stay up to date with new innovations and ensure tighter collaboration throughout the life cycle of the solution deployed to the customer. This will improve business outcomes and lead to higher retention rates and greater revenue opportunities for both the product company and its partners.

AI-Driven Value Management for Customer Success

We live in a world where customers increasingly call the shots and where "keeping the customer happy" is no longer a tired cliché but a serious business imperative for nearly every modern B2B enterprise.

The realization of the need to adopt a customer-centric mindset crept up on businesses in the last two decades, and even today many continue to operate on the premise that their customers—faced with the aggravation and costs of switching vendors and service providers—were content to be "locked in" for years.

In this chapter, we'll show how value management techniques and strategies enhanced by advanced AI solutions—including digital assistants and twins—can drive better outcomes for your business and your customers. Companies that follow this approach are experiencing reduced customer churn, improved customer satisfaction and loyalty scores, and greater lifetime revenue capture.

What Is Customer Success and Why You Should Care?

Let's start with one of the best definitions of customer success we've seen: *Customer success (CS) refers to a business practice and philosophy focused on ensuring customer satisfaction and achieving their desired outcomes throughout their entire relationship with the company.*

Among thriving enterprises today, customer success is no longer a mere business "function." It has become nothing short of a transformational movement. It's a proactive approach that goes beyond simply providing a product or service or even just helping customers learn how to use and adopt the product. CS is a mission-critical capability that empowers companies to retain existing customers, maximize their lifetime value, and achieve sustainable growth. And yes, value management and AI are now part of that story.

What led to this transformation? Not long ago, companies mainly focused on getting new customers and used aggressive marketing campaigns and sales tactics to win them over. But they soon confronted a harsh reality: the ever-steepening cost of customer acquisition. Studies by Gartner and other industry analysts have shown that customer acquisition costs (CACs) can be as much as five times higher than customer retention costs.[1] Moreover, customer churn—when your customers decide to abandon your product or service—is a risk constantly lurking in the shadows for most companies, and especially for SaaS companies whose business is based on providing web-based services that can be easily cancelled at the push of a button.

For these subscription-based companies, every lost customer represents not just lost revenue in the current year, but also from future renewals and upsells. A number of studies in the last two decades on the impact of churn reduction have come back with more or less the same conclusion: Even a small reduction in customer churn can double your customer lifetime value. For example, a 5 percent reduction in churn can lead to a staggering 125 percent increase in customer lifetime value over a period of 5 years and up to 95 percent increase in profitability.[2]

---

[1] https://www.serviceinstitute.com/service-excellence/7-ways-to-delight-and-retain-your-customers; https://www.huify.com/blog/acquisition-vs-retention-customer-lifetime-value
[2] *"Reduce your customer churn rate with these 5 proven strategies,"* WebEngage (https://webengage.com/blog/5-effective-proven-strategies-to-reduce-your-customer-churn-rate/#:~:text=A%205%25%20reduction%20in%20customer,to%20reduce%20the%20churn%20rate)

That's why customer success is not just relevant, but a top priority for nearly every enterprise. When done well, it sets in motion the much sought-after virtuous cycle of self-reinforcing business growth. When your CS teams work closely with customers to understand their needs, to onboard them effectively and ensure they're maximizing the value of your product or service, they ultimately create long-term, loyal customers that pay dividends over time. You've now moved beyond basic customer satisfaction and begin cultivating enduring strategic partnerships. These are customers that become vocal advocates for your business, generating positive word of mouth and entertaining new upselling opportunities. This virtuous cycle fosters long-term success for you and your customers.

"CUSTOMER SUCCESS" VS. "CUSTOMER SERVICE"

Customer success is more than just reacting to customer issues after they arise. It's a comprehensive strategy encompassing the entire customer journey, from onboarding and initial adoption to ongoing engagement and proactive churn prevention. While related, customer service is a more traditional term that focuses on reactive support. Customer service agents typically handle customer inquiries, troubleshoot issues, and resolve problems. Their primary goal is to address immediate customer needs and concerns. Some organizations may combine customer success and customer support, but for our purposes, we're going to use the conventional definition of customer success, which does not include the customer support or customer service function.

When you look at the high cost of customer acquisition and churn and compare it to the exponential value of retained customers, the value of customer success really stands out. With every business integrating some form of subscription into their business model, customer success has quickly become one of the most critical functions for every modern enterprise.

CUSTOMER SUCCESS AND CUSTOMER EXPERIENCE: TWO SIDES OF THE SAME COIN

Think of customer success (CS) and customer experience (CX) as two sides of the same coin, driving long-term customer satisfaction and loyalty. Whereas CX encompasses the entire customer journey, from initial awareness to post-purchase interactions, a significant portion—roughly 60–80 percent according to some studies—is directly influenced by CS efforts. Customer success managers (CSMs) become customer advocates, ensuring a smooth onboarding process, maximizing product value realization, and proactively addressing concerns. This translates to positive interactions, increased adoption, and ultimately, a great customer experience.

Now, you might ask what customer success has to do with value management. Well, it turns out that CS and value management are quite closely related. In fact, in our opinion, they should not just coexist but should be deeply integrated with each other. Here's why.

We often talk about *value realization*—a key phase in the life cycle of a customer. It's when customers capture and hopefully monetize the business value of the products and services they've invested in. That may sound like the goal of a value management practice—and it is. In fact, our take is that it is synonymous with customer success. We see customer success and business value realization as two sides of the same coin. While other functions like sales, professional services, and customer support play crucial roles in the customer journey, their interactions are often limited in scope and duration. Sales focuses on closing the deal, professional services might handle implementation, and support tackles specific issues. But the CS team has a unique opportunity for continuous engagement with the customer.

From onboarding and initial adoption through ongoing usage and value extraction, CSMs guide the customer's experience. This continuous involvement allows them to understand the customer's evolving needs and ensure they are maximizing the solution's potential, ultimately driving measurable business value for the customer—the very essence of customer success. This is one area where CS teams have faced challenges, mostly due to capacity constraints (which we will explore later in this chapter).

MEET NICK MEHTA AND GAINSIGHT: CUSTOMER SUCCESS PIONEERS

When it comes to building and managing a customer success program, few can match the vision and experience of Nick Mehta, founder and CEO of Gainsight, a world leader in helping businesses drive growth by improving customer engagement and retention. For over a decade, Mehta has tirelessly championed the customer success movement from its very inception. Gainsight's comprehensive platform has set industry standards, helping SaaS businesses extract product usage intelligence and customer sentiment to drive adoption, boost retention, and expand revenues.

Mehta is also a passionate advocate of incorporating value management in every customer-facing function of the business, including customer success programs. In our numerous conversations with him about the role of business value services in the customer life cycle, Mehta has pointed out that ultimately customer success is about value realization.

"Customer success can sometimes become too focused on adoption and retention. In other words, there is an undue emphasis placed on the vendor's outcomes," Mehta tells us. "This is going to sound obvious, but true customer success is about the customer's success. At Gainsight we have a more far-reaching definition of customer success, at whose heart is customer value realization."

For Mehta, customer success represents a business strategy focused on ensuring customers achieve their desired outcomes while using a vendor's product or service. "Customer success involves proactively managing and optimizing the customer life cycle to forecast value, drive adoption, drive satisfaction, realize value, retention, and growth—in that sequence," he says. "Customer success's most important consequence is value realization for customers, which ultimately will lead to the vendor's growth as well."

Understanding the Customer Success Workflow

How do customer success programs work inside the typical B2B or SaaS company? For both the CS team and the customer, it's a multipart journey. Let's do a quick end-to-end tour of the typical customer success journey.

1. **Pilot program support:**   When companies conduct a pilot program before the implementation, the CS team helps by assessing customer fit and ensuring users have a smooth initial experience with the pilot. Activities include monitoring key health indicators like pilot usage data and user sentiment to identify potential roadblocks early on. Regular check-ins with pilot users provide valuable insights that can help refine the solution's value proposition and ensure a successful implementation.

2. **Implementation:**   The implementation phase is when you set the stage for long-term success. CS teams actively participate even during the configuration of the solution and aim for a seamless transition from the professional services team to the CS team. Close monitoring of KPIs like system uptime and user adoption during implementation allows for timely adjustments and ensures the customer is on track to realize value quickly.

3. **Customer onboarding and reporting:** Customer onboarding is where CS teams shine, helping guide new customers through product familiarization and best practices and fostering early adoption. Continuous monitoring of KPIs like completion rates and time-to-first-value helps identify areas for improvement and ensures a smooth transition to the ongoing customer journey.

4. **Education:** Empowering users to leverage the solution's full potential is key to driving customer success. The CS team can provide ongoing education tailored to user needs including training sessions, workshops, or access to a resource knowledge base. By ensuring users are well equipped with necessary knowledge and skills, they can maximize the value they extract from the solution and achieve their desired outcomes.

5. **KPI reporting:** Regular performance reporting on customer success KPIs is essential for documenting the impact of CS efforts. These KPIs can encompass various metrics such as user adoption rates, time-to-value, customer satisfaction score (CSAT), and net promoter score (NPS). By tracking and reporting on these metrics, CS teams can communicate the value they deliver to their organization. Such performance tracking also allows for data-driven decision-making, enabling CS teams to continuously improve their strategies and optimize the customer experience.

6. **Adoption:** High adoption is crucial for customer success. CS teams monitor user activity and engagement to identify areas for improvement and proactively address any adoption roadblocks. Regular health checks ensure the customer continues to see value and identify potential churn risks early for timely intervention.

7. **Continuous customer health monitoring:** Continuous customer health monitoring involves monitoring key metrics, user activity, and sentiment to identify potential issues before they escalate. Regular check-ins with customers ensure they continue to see value from the solution and allow for early intervention if any churn risks are detected. By focusing on continuous health monitoring, CS teams can build stronger relationships, prevent churn, and foster long-term customer success.

8. **Value realization:** Of course, value realization is the ultimate goal of any customer success initiative. This involves quantifying and communicating value, combined with the process of delivering the maximum business value for customers using your product.

CS teams are at the center of this process, helping to demonstrate how your offering translates to concrete benefits like increased revenue, cost savings, or improved efficiency for their business.

VM PRO TIP

Once the deal is won and the contract is signed, bring your CS team to the forefront of the customer relationship, helping with onboarding, adoption, customer health, and more. It's when your customer uses your product that value is actually created. Every day, week, and month, value is being created in collaboration with the customer.

EMPOWERING CSMs WITH MODERN ENTERPRISE TOOLS

Customer success managers (CSMs) can use a variety of software systems to manage customer relationships and track progress. Here are some common enterprise systems used by CSMs and how they integrate across functions:

- **Customer relationship management (CRM) systems** serve as a central hub for storing customer data, interaction history, and communication records. CRM solutions integrate with the following:
  - *Salesforce automation (SFA) systems* ensure a smooth handoff from sales to customer success by providing insights into customer needs and initial conversations.
  - *Marketing automation systems* enable targeted communications based on customer segments and behavior.
  - *Support ticketing systems* allow for the seamless transition of support issues from CSMs to technical teams.
- **Customer success management platforms** provide tools for onboarding, managing customer health, tracking KPIs, and automating tasks:
  - *CRM systems* provide bidirectional data flow that ensures both systems have the most up-to-date customer information.
  - *Usage analytics tools* provide insights into customer behavior and feature adoption, informing customer success management outreach and value realization strategies.
  - *Value automation solutions* facilitate data extraction and analysis for value realization assessments.
- **Communication and collaboration tools** such as Slack and Microsoft Teams enable real-time communication and collaboration within the CS

team as well as with other departments like product, marketing, and engineering.

▪ **Data visualization and reporting tools** help CSMs create reports and dashboards showcasing customer success metrics and progress toward goals. They integrate with CRM and customer success management platforms, where data can be accessed directly for automated report generation.

Better Together: Combining Customer Success and Value Management

Whether you're a traditional brick-and-mortar business or a subscription-based SaaS company, it goes without saying that keeping customers happy is a must-have. But true success lies in demonstrating the tangible business value customers derive from your solution. That's why one of the most important tasks of CS teams is to collaborate with customers to track progress toward their business goals. When defining KPIs that align with the customer's business objectives, value management and business case concepts take center stage. By monitoring these KPIs and user behavior, CS teams can identify areas where the solution is delivering value and opportunities for further optimization. Ultimately, CS aims to secure a positive return on investment (ROI) for the customer. (See Figure 8.1 for how CS and value management boost customer lifetime value.)

Here's how value management practices can empower CS teams:

▪ **Targeted onboarding:** By understanding the customer's specific business goals, CS teams can tailor the onboarding process to highlight features directly relevant to those objectives. This increases adoption rates and sets the stage for early value realization.

▪ **Personalized engagement:** Customer data and insights from your value management program can enable CS teams to personalize interactions with customers, focusing on areas where the product can deliver the most significant impact on their business.

▪ **Proactive upselling and cross-selling:** VM insights help identify opportunities to recommend additional features or services that directly address customer needs and further enhance the value they derive from your product.

- **Reduced churn:** Customers who see and understand the tangible business value they receive from your solution are more likely to maintain their subscriptions and become long-term partners.

By integrating value management into your customer success strategy, you create a win-win situation. Customers see the concrete benefits of using your product, and your company benefits from increased customer retention and the associated revenue growth. By focusing on ensuring customer satisfaction and demonstrating the quantifiable business value customers receive, you create a powerful synergy that benefits both parties:

- **Your customers** experience a smooth onboarding process, receive personalized engagement that addresses their specific needs, and see tangible results that improve their bottom line. This fosters loyalty and a long-term commitment to your product.

- **Your company** reduces churn, translating to recurring revenue and increased customer lifetime value. Additionally, by aligning product development with customer needs identified through VM, you can ensure that your offering continues to deliver value and remain competitive in the market.

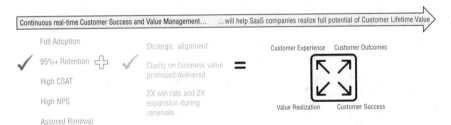

Figure 8.1:   Maximizing customer lifetime value through customer success and value management

This combined approach can empower CS teams to move beyond reactive support and elevate their role to become strategic partners with their customers. The following section discusses the challenges that teams face in their effort to fully realize this potential.

The Challenge of Integrating Value Management and Customer Success

Although we see growing awareness of the value that companies can create by integrating value management and customer success practices, most CS teams face an uphill battle when trying to make that vision a reality. The key stumbling block: the lack of bandwidth, skills, and tools that CSMs need to understand and leverage value management concepts in their day-to-day jobs.

For example, the average CSM may have little experience in forecasting the business value of implementing new features or products. Consequently, many struggle to set clear expectations with customers on what business value they should expect to see. Ideally, CS teams would quantify expected value right after the contract is signed, employing a proven business value assessment tool to set a common direction for both the implementation and the CS teams. (In reality, this tends to require the help of expensive consultants.) Stepping into an implementation and onboarding project without a value forecast on the table hides unexpressed expectations and introduces risk.

An exceptional CSM should be able to look beyond traditional customer success KPIs—such as basic user adoption and satisfaction numbers—and learn to incorporate business value metrics backed by the ability to forecast, measure, and report it in meaningful ways to different audiences. Here again, value management comes to the fore as a necessary skill. However, as you might imagine, delivering value realization along with continuous value forecasting, tracking, and messaging can be an enormously expensive undertaking. It's akin to having a value management team at the CS team's disposal on a continuous basis.

Pressures Mount for Customer Success Teams

With CS programs recently facing tighter executive scrutiny and fixed budgets, it has become harder to secure funding for the tools, technologies, and training needed to include value-based deliverables as part of their job responsibilities. Meanwhile, customer bases continue to grow, putting pressure on CSMs to add more customers to their workload and making it more difficult to maintain highly personalized customer engagements. In this environment, CSMs are less likely to find the time to integrate value management into their regular job duties.

Increasingly, companies are focusing on identifying at-risk customers early enough to prevent churn. This, too, requires deep value realization assessments—and not just at the time of renewal but throughout the customer life cycle. For CSMs, such robust data analysis and proactive engagement strategies require more bandwidth, not less.

Remember that data is at the core of value realization, and for CS teams, tracking down the right data can be a formidable task when it resides in different siloed systems across the organization, preventing a holistic view of the customer and limiting the effectiveness of data-driven CS initiatives. Compared to sales-oriented value assessments conducted in the early stages of the sales cycle, longer-term value realization assessments developed by CS teams can be far more data intensive.

VM PRO TIP

When value forecasts during the marketing and sales cycles diverge significantly from value assessments conducted later during the customer success phases, it can lead to unrealistic customer expectations regarding the product's capabilities and value proposition. Make sure all three teams are in alignment or CS teams may have to bear the brunt of overly optimistic value forecasts made during the sales cycle.

The CSM's Toughest Challenge: Measuring and Communicating Value

Ideally, every customer success manager should be able to quantify and communicate the business value realized by the customer—and they should do this:

- In the business language of the customer
- At every key moment throughout the customer life cycle, whether it is weekly, monthly, or quarterly
- In terms of operational, functional, strategic, and financial value
- Following an executive storytelling format (such as "Objectives–Challenges–Capabilities–Outcomes")
- Comparing before-and-after customer workflows
- Comparing before-and-after performance metrics
- Briefly—such as during a 15-minute conversation with the customer, showing before-and-after workflows
- More in depth—such as during a quarterly business review or annual review that includes ROI analysis, cash flow, and cost savings

Are we asking too much from the CSM on value messaging? Perhaps. It's true that CS organizations face serious constraints when they try to integrate value measurement messaging into their operations. Most notably, few CSMs have spare bandwidth to devote to time-consuming business value analyses. Plus, few have the required skills or experience in business consulting or value management. Finally, while CSMs often need to collaborate with value engineers or consultants in the sales organization to put together value messaging and analyses, the same is not true for sales teams. Instead, they are focused on winning deals and renewals and have little incentive to help CSMs with ongoing value realization projects.

However, CS teams do have some options to help uplevel their value messaging:

- Hire value management consultants within the CS organization who will work hand in hand with the CSMs. Even if this service is targeted only for the largest and most strategic customers, this approach can increase the cost of the customer success operation. Some companies position this as a "value realization service" and charge customers a fee.

- Train CSMs on value management concepts such as customer discovery, strategy mapping, and ROI analysis. As explained earlier, "full suite" value skills present a steep learning curve for CSMs and is akin to creating another core competency.

- Create value content and tools that CSMs can access on their own. This self-service approach will help alleviate some of their trouble, but it still requires a high level of value analysis skills on the part of the CSMs.

Table 8.1 describes the various skills that customer success managers need to master to communicate business value effectively.

Table 8.1: Upskilling CSMs: The starting point for creating effective business value messaging

VALUE SKILL	EFFORT AND COMPLEXITY LEVEL FOR CSMs	CONTRIBUTION TO CS VALUE MESSAGING
How to discover/research customer business, functional, and operational objectives	Simple	High
How to speak the customer's business language (value taxonomy)	Simple	High

VALUE SKILL	EFFORT AND COMPLEXITY LEVEL FOR CSMs	CONTRIBUTION TO CS VALUE MESSAGING
How to define customer workflows and metrics	Medium	High
How to identify key "value moments" that represent value and build value moments	Simple	High
How to do cash flow and ROI analysis	Complex	Low
How to do strategic value advisory; e.g., create strategy maps, phased road maps, SWOT analysis	Complex	Low
Value selling skills	Complex	High
Negotiation	Complex	High
Orchestration for value	Complex	High

Touchpoints: Where Value Management Meets Customer Success

One reason why it's so hard for customer success and sales-based value management teams to collaborate effectively is that they're out of sync when it comes to the demand for and frequency of their services during the customer life cycle. For example, we can summarize the value management team's involvement in the customer life cycle at two "touchpoints": once during pre-sales and once at renewal.

- In the pre-sales phase, VM consultants help forecast the value they will get, helping customers justify the investment.
- During the renewal phase, they measure the value realized, helping secure renewals.

In specific cases the VM team may engage to provide strategic value services to the customer to propose new ideas and build pipeline. Note that, unlike customer success teams, VM consultants in the sales organization create and deliver value messaging at discrete points in time and not continually. The disconnect between the two groups can lead to missed chances for forging stronger customer bonds and boosting lifetime customer value.

Figure 8.2 presents a comprehensive summary of the mission, services, roles, engagement methods, and success measures of the two organizations. Note the "point-in-time" involvement of value management teams and near-continuous involvement of CS teams.

MASTERING THE ART AND SCIENCE OF VALUE MANAGEMENT

It can be daunting for the average customer success manager to incorporate value management techniques into their everyday work life. For one, it requires skills beyond traditional customer support, such as data analysis and storytelling abilities. Plus, it adds another layer of work to the CSM's already overcrowded plate of customer calls, onboarding, and issue resolution.

"Customer success should be the home of value management," says Gainsight's Nick Mehta. "But the reality is that while CS teams are great at driving usage, adoption, retention, and even revenue expansion, they often come up short on communicating the value in a business or executive language. Many customer success teams don't just have the bandwidth to include value management in their ever-expanding list of things to do, and many simply don't have either the skillset or toolset—and in some cases the mindset—for creating value narratives."

AI: Changing the Customer Success Game

Like in many other parts of the business, AI-powered tools and technologies are beginning to transform customer success teams, empowering them to remove organizational barriers, automate manual processes, and speed the realization of business results. Let's first take a look at how AI-driven customer success programs can deliver actionable insights faster than ever and free up CSMs to focus on what matters: helping customers realize the business value they've paid for.

Automating Customer Success

AI-powered chatbots and virtual assistants, already increasingly common in the customer service world, will grow in popularity among customer success teams, providing basic customer support around the clock, answering frequently asked questions, troubleshooting routine issues, and directing customers to relevant resources. Repetitive tasks like data entry, report generation, and scheduling follow-up emails can be automated using AI. That means CS teams will have more time for complex customer interactions such as value discovery and analysis.

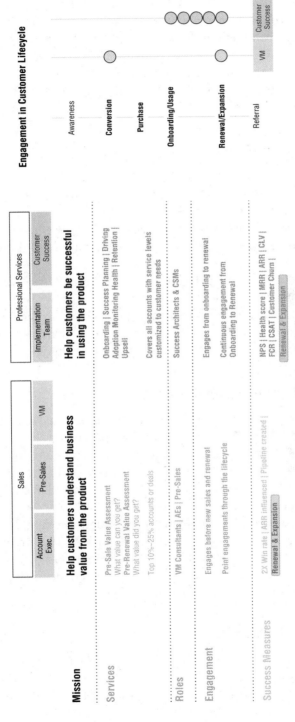

Figure 8.2: Customer success and value management organizational challenges

Similarly, AI tools can help CS teams personalizing the onboarding experience for new customers by tailoring content and recommendations based on customer data and user preferences that are progressively "learned" and refined by AI assistants and increasingly aligned with the customer's business goals. Leveraging this automation, CSMs get a head start an engaging the customer and aligning with their strategy objectives.

Harnessing Data

By mining customer data with AI, customer success teams can rapidly segment their customers according to usage patterns, business goals, and other relevant factors. This enables CS teams to tailor their value messaging, engagement strategies, and content to the specific needs of each customer group and subgroup, helping cultivate a more personalized relationship.

Number crunching will get a lot easier with AI. Not long ago, complex value realization assessments were limited to large or at-risk renewals because of the volume of data crunching needed. AI can analyze massive datasets to uncover hidden patterns and extract actionable insights that wouldn't be readily apparent through manual analysis.

Driving Sales and Loyalty

Value realization is not just about reporting value realized—it's also about highlighting new value opportunities. AI-powered recommendation engines can analyze customer usage data to recommend relevant features, resources, and upsell/cross-sell opportunities that directly address individual customer needs—and lift the top lines of B2B companies.

Want to boost customer loyalty? By using AI to analyze customer interaction data, CS teams can identify areas for improving the customer journey. CS teams can now optimize touchpoints and create a more seamless customer experience that can inspire long-term loyalty. Viewed from a value realization perspective, these may be the touchpoints that most benefit from targeted value messaging.

Capturing Greater Value

CS teams are in a great position know when customers might be underutilizing product features or not experiencing the full potential value of a solution. To confirm these suspicions, CSMs need to analyze vast amounts of customer usage data—and AI assistants trained for this task stand ready to help. CS teams can now proactively engage with customers and suggest solutions that bridge these value gaps.

Indeed, the best AI models can quantify business value customers derived from your solution in granular detail across multiple financial and operating domains. The wealth of data can help you communicate the ROI of your product more effectively and demonstrate its impact on customer success. What's more, we are seeing AI-powered churn prediction models that can analyze customer behavior and feedback data to identify early warning signs of dissatisfaction. This allows CS teams to proactively intervene with tailored support and allay customer concerns before they lead to churn.

BULLISH ON AI-DRIVEN CS

Given the value-creating potential of AI we've just reviewed, it's no surprise that Gainsight's Nick Mehta is bullish on the transformative power of AI for customer success programs. "CS is being reimagined as we speak with a new wave of AI capabilities," Mehta tells us. Gainsight's product always had lots of AI built into it, whether it's for predicting customer health, anomalies, churn risk, upsell opportunities, or designing new customer interactions and work-flows. But with the advent of generative AI, Gainsight has been introducing a host of new features, including automated content generation, conversational AI, and customer insights—all tailored for the specific customer the team is working with.

Gainsight also uses AI to simulate various customer scenarios and outcomes, which helps businesses plan and optimize their customer success strategies. "Everything has value realization at its core," explains Nick. He sees a near-future where customer success managers are accompanied by AI assistants who are skilled in helping them have the value conversation. Today, Nick continues to use his significant influence and reach within the high-tech industry to champion the need for a convergence of value management and customer success.

Raising the Performance Bar with AI

Table 8.2 shows how customer success KPIs can be boosted through business value measurement (BVM) and messaging, the challenges faced, how AI can address those challenges, and the expected improvement for each KPI.

Table 8.2: Impact of value management and AI on KPIs

KEY PERFORMANCE INDICATOR (KPI)	HOW VALUE MESSAGING BOOSTS THE KPI	CHALLENGES	AI USE CASES	EXPECTED KPI BOOST
Customer Value Realization (CVR)	Aligns customer needs with solution benefits, demonstrating ongoing value	Difficulty in quantifying value, lack of clear value messaging	Analyzes customer data to identify value drivers, generates personalized value reports and success stories	5–10% increase
Customer Retention Rate (CRR)	Ensures customers understand value attained improves retention	Difficulty in quantifying value can make solution impact opaque	Automate and scale CVR reports to all customers in advance of a renewal	10–15% increase
Customer Lifetime Value (CLTV)	Encourages upselling/cross-selling by showcasing additional value opportunities	Limited visibility into customer usage patterns, difficulty in identifying upsell /cross-sell potential	Analyzes usage data to predict future needs, recommends relevant features/services	10–15% increase
Net Promoter Score (NPS)	Increases customer satisfaction through clear value communication and exceeding expectations	Difficulty in translating value into relatable metrics for customers	Uses sentiment analysis to understand customer perceptions, personalizes communication based on value realization	10–15 point increase
Time-to-Value (TTV)	Streamlines onboarding by focusing on features that deliver immediate value	Lack of data-driven insights into user adoption patterns	Analyzes user behavior to identify roadblocks, personalizes onboarding based on user goals	20–30% reduction in TTV

KEY PERFORMANCE INDICATOR (KPI)	HOW VALUE MESSAGING BOOSTS THE KPI	CHALLENGES	AI USE CASES	EXPECTED KPI BOOST
Net Promoter Score (NPS)	Identifies proclivity to recommend your solution to other customers	Challenge to understand why a customer may not feel comfortable recommending your solution	Analyzes customer data to pinpoint any value-related challenges a customer may have experienced	5–10 point increase
Customer Satisfaction Score (CSAT)	Proactive issue resolution and addressing concerns before dissatisfaction arises	Difficulty in identifying at-risk customers and potential pain points	Analyzes customer interactions and usage data to predict churn risk, enables proactive interventions	5–10 point increase

A DAY IN THE LIFE OF A CUSTOMER SUCCESS MANAGER

The typical day of a customer success manager is a blend of proactive planning and reactive support. The morning might involve checking key customer health metrics and planning outreach for at-risk accounts. Then, it's on to calls—onboarding new customers, ensuring existing ones are successful, and troubleshooting issues. The afternoon could be spent crafting success plans, collaborating with product or sales teams, and analyzing data to identify upsell opportunities. It's a fast-paced role that requires juggling priorities but ultimately focuses on building relationships and ensuring customer satisfaction.

The Future of AI-Powered Customer Success

The future of AI-driven customer success is full of possibilities, from more sophisticated personalization of the customer journey to faster and better customer recommendations. We envision AI-powered chatbots and virtual assistants becoming increasingly more sophisticated, empowering customers to find answers and resolve issues on their own with jaw-dropping speed. We see AI tools that get progressively better at predicting customer needs and proactively addressing them before they become issues. And we're expecting the latest customer success platforms, augmented by AI, to become even more tightly integrated with other business systems (CRM, marketing automation) and able to generate a truly holistic view of the customer.

Madhav Thattai, COO of Salesforce AI, a division of the SaaS giant, is well situated to see the emerging landscape of AI and customer success, having also served as the COO for Salesforce's Customer Success group. Salesforce, as many of you know, is one of the world's most admired SaaS companies when it comes to CRM, but you may not know that the company is also an innovator in value management and customer success.

From the perspective of a customer success practitioner, Thattai told us he likes to "broaden the definition of value" and look "beyond the numbers" and include other "value dimensions" such as:

- Does the product work at scale, and is it always on and effective in what it does?

- Is it well adopted? Does it have active engagement, and are we grooming super users?

- Do we have quantifiable proof points that the customer (that works with the CS team) can relate to?

Thattai implemented this expanded value playbook when he led the company's customer success group, noting that the approach is "tailored to the nature of the customer success function, which is the only function that is continuously involved with the customer and therefore is in a unique position to communicate value to the customer, and particularly the users."

Wearing his AI hat, Thattai connects the dots between customer success, business value, and AI: "Gone are the days when customer feature requests would have to trickle back to product teams with months to years of development effort. AI workflows can easily stitch together and deliver the feature in a systems integration mode—rather than a product development mode. Time from promise to delivery has never been shorter! AI is thus providing a template for much quicker realization of these features (and thus related benefits), accelerating customer-focused product development. The importance of value management has never been higher."

AI capabilities have been rapidly evolving even as we write the book. Specifically for customer success and value management functions, Thattai outlines "three modes of AI" we can leverage:

- Reactive (responding to user requests for information or actions)
- Proactive (time-based or event-based actions driven by AI)
- Autonomous AI (actions based on complex rules, some or all of which are independently executed by AI agents that plan and collaborate with each other)

In particular, Thattai believes that autonomous AI (or agentic AI) can solve the resourcing challenges that are involved with value research and articulation—whether it is for customer success or value management.

Over the last several chapters, we have taken you on a tour of marketing, sales, professional services, and customer success. We are strong advocates of creating a companywide value program, but before anyone gets there, value management has to be integrated into the domain of customer success. With AI, this is now a financially viable and technically possible goal.

In the next chapter, we will bring it all together and lay out our vision of how a companywide value management program powered by AI might look.

One Value Motion: The Power of Unified Value Management

So far, this book has shown how AI-driven customer value management can be a game changer for every part of the B2B enterprise and for ecosystem partners. We've delved into the people, processes, and technologies necessary to build a mature value management practice, from marketing and sales to customer success and retention.

We've also shown how AI technologies can overcome the challenges companies face as they seek to implement and grow their value management practices and achieve greater efficiencies, cost savings, and revenue. We've documented how AI-VM strategies deliver significant business and customer outcomes throughout the customer life cycle and for each functional area. Indeed, we are seeing companies realize 2X sales performance increases by adopting AI-VM programs.

However, the reality is that implementing an AI-driven value management program in a piecemeal fashion—that is, one business function at a time—only gets you partway there.

The Journey to a Unified Enterprise

In this chapter we argue that to achieve the full growth potential in sales pipeline (lead generation), win rates, and customer expansion (retention), companies will need to embrace AI-driven value management on an enterprisewide scale and achieve buy-in at the highest level of executive leadership. The goal: to establish a unified value management system by bringing together every business function in a coordinated way to help customers realize even greater business value. It's a strategic concept and an operational framework that we call *One Value Motion*.

To be sure, we've found many individual business functions that have made good progress toward building a mature value management program. Sales organizations usually lead the way because value management programs have a direct impact on sales outcomes. Sales executives are naturally inclined to adopt practices that directly influence their ability to close deals and drive revenue, making them the ideal starting point for value management initiatives.

As sales teams continue to experience tangible benefits from their value-driven initiatives, their success breeds more success, providing a compelling reason for extending these practices to other functions in the company, such as marketing and customer success. However, the ability to extend these programs to other groups can be hampered by several factors, including:

- **Turf battles:** Some organizations, such as marketing or customer success, may resist having sales change any of the activities they own or mandate new processes.

- **Unrealistic expectations and minimal oversight:** Simply handing over complex value management tools (such as complex ROI value models) to other functions can be met by inaction or poor user adoption.

- **Lack of tools:** Deploying value management programs requires tools that help automate and structure the quantification and communication of value to customers and ecosystem partners. Often, the tooling that sales teams use to communicate value can't be easily extended to marketing and customer success teams.

Compared to sales organizations, marketing and customer success functions often find it harder to measure the impact of adopting value management practices. For example, specific business outcomes—such as increased brand awareness, lead generation, customer satisfaction, and customer retention—typically lack the direct linkage to revenue generation that the sales organization sees.

For example, marketing teams might use value management insights to craft compelling messaging and go-to-market campaigns, but the impact on revenue is realized over a longer time horizon and can be influenced by many other factors beyond just value management. Similarly, customer success functions are focused on ensuring that customers realize business value post-purchase, but the link between these efforts and long-term customer retention or share of wallet expansion is often more nuanced and difficult to attribute directly to value management activities.

Thus, marketers and customer success managers (CSMs) may turn to value management for some needs but not others. A few examples include:

- **Marketing PR efforts:** Value management can play a critical role in customer messaging, but the placement and promotion of a solution is not directly related to value management programs.

- **Marketing events and conferences:** Value management can help create messaging that resonates with prospective buyers but is not involved in other aspects of a successful event or conference.

- **Customer success service improvements:** Many customer success teams rely on value management techniques to document business outcomes and ensure customers are realizing value (and likely to renew or buy new products). But value management approaches are less likely to be useful in operationalizing or integrating products within the customer's environment.

WHEN PRODUCT MARKETING TAKES THE LEAD IN VALUE MANAGEMENT

Are sales organizations always the first to implement value management programs? Not necessarily. We discovered a global cybersecurity company in which its product marketing team took the initiative, launching its own value management program and then seeking support for it across the other business groups.

The team created a set of *value trees* (a structured model of value drivers, KPIs, and benchmarks) and a sophisticated ROI model that the company's marketing, sales, channel partners, and customer success teams could use for their go-to-market activities.

> Although it had limited resources, the product marketing team made impressive progress toward putting business value at the center of its product launch efforts and was pleased to share its value models and tools with other parts of the business. It even piloted its business case tools with the sales organization to prove their effectiveness at attracting and securing customers. Subsequently, sales funded a full-fledged value management program.

By contrast, value management practices are deeply intertwined with every stage of the sales process. From initial customer engagement to closing deals and driving expansions, value management acts as a critical enabler, providing the insights, tools, and frameworks needed to articulate the business value of a company's offerings in ways that resonate with customers. It's no wonder that sales tends to play the role as the "value custodian," whereas marketing and customer success organizations tend to experience slower value management adoption and achieve only a modest level of sophistication.

Unfortunately, with sales acting as the sole custodian of value—combined with the siloed nature of business functions and AI capabilities—the goal of a unified and seamless value management experience across the entire enterprise remains elusive. Figure 9.1 shows how multiple functional business silos can lead to fragmented value management activities across the enterprise.

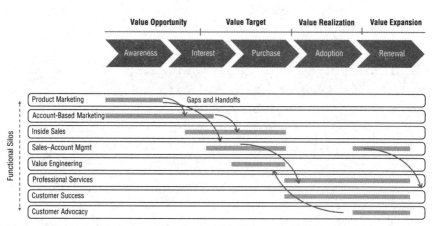

Value Management Steps × Customer Life cycle × Functional Activity

Figure 9.1:   Functional silos prevent a unified value management experience across the enterprise

Let's summarize the challenges of creating a unified value management system.

Sloppy Handoffs and Broken Workflows

It's no surprise that transferring business value messaging and content from one functional team to the next can lead to miscommunication and crossed wires, as operational silos impede the seamless flow of value intelligence between sales, marketing, customer success, and other business groups. Inefficient handoffs of key value management deliverables—everything from ROI business cases and customer success stories to notes taken during a customer value discovery workshop—can result in duplicated efforts and missed opportunities for leveraging insights across the company. Disconnected or poorly integrated workflows can also cause delays and errors, negatively impacting the enterprise value management process and risking damaging trust between teams.

TALE OF TWO CUSTOMER STORIES

What is the advantage of One Value Motion? We recently came across this "tale of two customer stories" at one of the world's largest enterprise companies. It turns out that its marketing and sales organizations had separately invested in value management programs and had created well-defined services and content deliverables for their respective operations.

The value management team working in the sales group created a series of assets it called the *Customer Value Story* consisting of an easy-to-read narrative of the customer's journey using data from a value realization assessment conducted just before the contract renewal deadline.

The marketing team also created a series of deliverables called simply the *Customer Story*, which relied on interviews with selected customers and was used on marketing's website and at events and customer engagements. The sales team's customer value story was rich in value-based KPIs and ROI insights, which the marketing story lacked. The marketing team, meanwhile, enjoyed the services of top tech writers, making its storytelling superior to that of sales, but it was hampered by limited customer data.

Making matters worse, the company's knowledge management system contained both stories, so when account executives searched for a Customer Story, they weren't sure which version to use or how to reconcile any discrepancies between the two stories. This is a good example of the benefit of creating a One Value Motion throughout the enterprise.

Differences in Taxonomy

Since each business function may use its own terminology and metrics to define and measure value, inconsistencies easily arise that can derail productive collaboration and data sharing. Chapter 2, "The Current State of Value Management," provides useful value management concepts and terms you can use when setting up a value management program (see also the Glossary).

WHEN TAXONOMY CAN FEEL LIKE A TAX

When the value management practice at a leading SaaS company decided to coin the term "Strategic Value Road Map" to describe its sales organization's planning activities, confusion reigned. The problem: The company's consulting organization and its customer success organization also had deliverables called "Road Maps" with the words "Strategic" and "Value" in their product names, such as Strategic Business Road Map, Customer Value Roadmap, and Strategic Road Map. Beyond these nomenclature overlaps, there were also duplications in project scope that created extra work and sparked conflicts between teams that had been assigned to work collaboratively on customer deals. What a mess!

Project teams at another leading technology provider used slightly different words to translate technical features into business capabilities and customer business outcomes. Reaching a consensus around terms such as productivity, speed, throughput, efficiency, agility, and cost avoidance added costly delays to the project.

VM PRO TIP

Creating consistent taxonomy of terms across the enterprise can help ensure alignment across functions, reduce redundant work, and drive dependable customer outcomes across the buyer journey.

Prioritization Conflicts

Different business functions may prioritize value management activities based on their individual goals, potentially creating a misalignment in efforts that fail to support the broader company's strategic objectives. For example, marketing may prioritize creating a lead-generation tool that delivers a value benefits message for a solution at the same time that sales launches a business case tool to support ROI measurement, but these two provide very different value quantifications to the customer.

Success Measures

Variability in how value management program success is defined and measured across functions can lead to disjointed strategies and outcomes. One example that we found was for a global high-tech company that measured the impact of business cases for sales but didn't measure the ability to deliver on the business cases by the customer success team, which was measuring only risk of renewal based on license consumption. This disconnect on measuring business value created a gap in identifying renewal risk for customers that were turning on licenses but not adopting the business use cases defined in the business case.

Governance Gaps

Inconsistent governance structures across functions can create a lack of accountability and coordination, leading to fragmented value management initiatives. This is a very common challenge for many B2B companies. A frequent challenge is when marketing hands qualified leads generated from a value lead-gen tool that ends up in a black hole with the inside sales team. The new marketing-to-sales motion of providing a qualified lead with a value proposition already defined requires new business processes to be stood up and training to be delivered to manage effectively.

WHO OWNS CUSTOMER VALUE REALIZATION?

B2B companies naturally want to know how much business value their customers are getting from the products and services they've invested in. That's where a formal *value realization assessment* (see the Glossary) can help, and it's often a must-have for companies trying to secure customer renewals and increase wallet share. Today, customer success organizations typically "own" the customer renewal process, which makes sense because customer success organizations—increasingly bolstered by a value management team—are well positioned to conduct these assessments.

But the sales organization can also get involved and commission their own assessments, and there's a case to be made that a value management consultant within the sales organization should lead the way. When both a contract renewal and customer expansion (upsell/cross-sell) opportunities are involved (as is typically the case), or if the value realization service is a for-fee service (as part of a customer success service), the question of who owns the value assessment effort can get complicated.

To avoid stepping on each other's toes, sales and customer success organizations need to agree on decision-making criteria and workflows that will align and drive collaboration between the teams. Without establishing shared roles and responsibilities, the company will have a hard time achieving value-management-at-scale.

VM PRO TIP

Close integration between sales and customer success teams is essential for building a One Value Motion culture at B2B enterprises. For example, sales teams can benefit from insights collected by customer success teams as they track customer outcomes post-implementation, which can inform the sales team's customer retention and upsell opportunities.

Functional vs. Enterprisewide AI Approaches

AI plays a pivotal role in helping enterprises automate and scale their operations. But if each business department or function chooses to develop its own AI capability, it may lead to separate AI "silos" that can slow the progress of AI initiatives that could have benefited the whole company. To get the most out of a unified enterprise AI-VM approach, AI solutions must be *deeply embedded* into enterprisewide workflows and integrated across the customer's journey in a holistic fashion.

Table 9.1 summarizes value management program results across three levels of maturity: early stage, standard, and at-scale.

Table 9.1:   Value management programs across maturity stages

	EARLY STAGE	STANDARD	AT-SCALE
Funnel Impact	None/Marginal	Top 50 accounts	Across all accounts
Revenue Growth	Few deals	Limited uplift	2 to the power of 3
Win Rate	Few deals	2X improvement	2X improvement
Churn Rate	A few segments	2X reduction	2X reduction

	EARLY STAGE	STANDARD	AT-SCALE
Share of Wallet	No impact	Limited increase	2X increase
CSAT	No impact	Improvement	Improvement
Margins	No impact	Deal margin improvement	Deal margin improvement
Outcomes	Low	Medium	High

Solving the Puzzle of an Enterprisewide Value Management Program

Unifying value management programs across a multibillion-dollar B2B company can be a daunting assignment. We liken it to solving a massively complex jigsaw puzzle: Once all the pieces are put in the proper place, a complete picture of an enterprisewide value management program emerges. It's a meticulous process, but it brings greater value to the enterprise than the individual parts on their own.

Before the advent of generative AI, we participated in similarly complex business-transformation projects in which we successfully brought together multiple department-based value management programs. We did this primarily by designing workflows that bridged the gaps between operational silos and created organizational overlays and automation tools that connected people, processes, and technologies. Working at one of the world's most admired SaaS companies, the unification took more than three years and required millions of dollars in value management investments.

To our delight, the benefits realized by the company were enormous, proving our thesis that value management programs, done properly, can deliver "2-to-the-power-of-3" in financial returns. In this book, we have attempted to take our thesis a step further by showing how AI will help unify disparate operational groups and help achieve this goal at a much lower cost than traditional approaches.

Creating One Value Motion: A Unified Value Management Framework

What if all your go-to-market functions, from marketing to sales to customer success (and don't forget your partner ecosystem) could act as a single point of contact for each customer? As previously mentioned, this hypothetical, singular customer contact dedicated to each customer can now become reality by implementing a unified value management framework that we call *One Value Motion*.

This "single voice-of-value" would transform the customer experience by providing a consistent and reinforcing set of value messages that is proven to resonate with each customer across its buying journey. Importantly, the framework will ensure streamlined interactions between customers and vendors as they make critical buying and renewal decisions. Customers will no longer get frustrated finding the right person to talk to, they'll always get detailed and accurate answers to questions about the products or business issues they're interested in (or currently using), and they are regularly updated on the business outcomes they're achieving.

By implementing One Value Motion, companies leverage a singular value resource for each customer by integrating and unifying value management processes across all business functions and the partner ecosystem. It will help customers realize exceptional value from their investments, and reward the company with exceptional pipeline, revenue, retention, and customer expansion outcomes.

Achieving One Value Motion requires a comprehensive, enterprise value management framework that brings together a common vision driven by a common set of value management tools, content, services, and success measures. It's a coordinated, companywide approach, infused by value management tools and technologies, that maximizes customer outcomes while optimizing internal operations and resources.

As companies roll out One Value Motion, they can start integrating AI tools and solutions to automate key elements of the initiative and drive cost efficiencies. As we noted previously, in order for AI to become a unifying value management force, it needs to be deeply integrated into the business workflows that underpin and automate the One Value Motion platform. At the time we are writing book, most AI tools and applications are just being piloted by enterprises, but already we have discovered several promising examples of AI's potential impact on B2B businesses and their customers. We are using these early AI use cases as a template to demonstrate how the One Value Motion framework could be implemented in the near future.

The One Value Motion Playbook

Whether you're a large enterprise with a relatively mature value management function or a small company in the early stages of adopting value management, we've created this One Value Motion Playbook to guide your teams as they implement a unified, enterprisewide value management platform.

Let's start by outlining specific executive and strategic actions that will need to be taken to launch your own One Value Motion initiative, the technologies and implementation requirements for setting up and scaling the platform (see Figure 9.2).

One Value Motion Initiative Playbook

Figure 9.2:   One Value Motion Playbook

Step 1: Define Your One Value Motion Mission

Think of One Value Motion as a significant corporate initiative that you deploy as a *horizontal service capability* for all your go-to-market business functions and partners with the goal of unifying all value management activities to achieve enterprise scale at minimal cost. The first step in launching your One Value Motion initiative should be to define its mission for your company. Drafting your mission statement should be straight-forward, and you can lean on the value management themes presented in this book. Here are two examples of a mission statement for a One Value Motion initiative:

> Unify and synchronize all business functions to maximize our cus-tomers' abilities to achieve their business objectives and realize exceptional business outcomes.

> Optimize our value management practices across all business functions, ensuring that every customer receives exceptional value throughout their life cycle with our company.

Step 2: Set the One Value Motion Strategy and Leadership Alignment

To justify the initiative, the executive management team will need to make One Value Motion one of the top priorities of the company and embrace the goal of achieving or exceeding the customers' expected business outcomes needs. Executives need to articulate a clear and compelling mission for One Value Motion. The initiative's strategic intent should be clear:

- Our customers' business outcomes are a priority for the entire company and are a focus of the board of directors and our shareholders.

- By implementing a One Value Motion approach, our company will be rewarded with exceptional revenue growth and customer loyalty.

- Value management must be the responsibility of the entire leadership team and will measure KPIs that will be reviewed on a quarterly basis as part of the company's performance review process.

Step 3: Define Success Measures and Business Outcomes

The One Value Motion initiative represents a significant shift in go-to-market activities that will touch nearly every part of the enterprise. Tracking the program's performance across business functions will be essential for gauging its success or failure. So, you'll want to establish performance measures that track results of the program, such as revenues, prospect conversion rates, deal win rates, and churn rates. Many of these KPIs are well known and easy to adopt, and quickly gain executive buy-in. Here are a couple of examples of relevant value-management KPIs:

- **Sales funnel leading KPIs:** Biweekly tracking of sales volume, customer deal value, and percentage of customer deals covered/not covered by value management efforts.

- **Customer lifetime value KPIs:** Estimates of total life cycle value for a customer and improvements over time as VM efforts identify and capture cross-sell and upsell opportunities.

Step 4: Establish a Companywide Value Lexicon

Creating a consistent and standard lexicon for value-related concepts ensures that everyone is speaking the same language when it comes to value management. This is important because value management is typically a homegrown practice and can lead to the use of similar value terms that mean slightly different things to different organizations. When multiplied across functions, these terms can be confusing—not only to teams within the company, but more importantly to customers. This can slow the pace of deals, make for unnecessary rework, or even confuse customers to the point where they look elsewhere for solutions.

One way to translate product features into capabilities and business outcomes while keeping everything aligned is by deploying a *business capability framework* (see Table 9.2) to clarify and standardize these terms while interacting with customers.

Table 9.2:   Business capability framework example

PRODUCT FEATURE	PRODUCT CAPABILITY	BUSINESS OUTCOME
Real-Time Inventory Alerts	Immediate notification of low stock or excess inventory	Reduced stockouts, optimized inventory management
Automated Invoice Matching	Ensuring purchase orders and invoices match automatically	Reduced payment errors, faster accounts payable processing
Dynamic Content Personalization	Customizing web and email content based on user behavior	Increased engagement, higher conversion rates
Version History Tracking	Detailed record of changes made to documents	Improved document accuracy, enhanced auditability
Sales Activity Logging	Automatic recording of sales interactions	Better sales tracking, improved customer engagement
Supplier Scorecarding	Performance evaluation of suppliers based on predefined criteria	Enhanced supplier management, improved procurement efficiency
Timesheet Auto-Approval	Automatically approving timesheets based on predefined rules	Streamlined payroll processing, reduced administrative overhead
Lead Routing Automation	Automatically assigning leads to the appropriate sales rep	Faster lead follow-up, improved lead conversion rates
Single Sign-On (SSO)	Unified login for multiple enterprise applications	Improved user experience, enhanced security compliance

Table 9.2: (continued)

PRODUCT FEATURE	PRODUCT CAPABILITY	BUSINESS OUTCOME
Workflow Triggered Notifications	Alerts triggered by specific workflow events	Increased operational efficiency, reduced delays
Automated Order Confirmation Emails	Immediate email confirmation upon order placement	Improved customer satisfaction, reduced order errors
Audit Trail for User Access	Tracking who accessed what and when	Enhanced security, compliance with data protection regulations
Change Request Automation	Automatically processing and routing change requests	Faster change implementation, reduced project delays
Direct Deposit Configuration	Automated setup of employee direct deposit accounts	Reduced payroll errors, increased employee satisfaction
Document Access Control	Restricting document access based on user roles	Enhanced data security, compliance with confidentiality requirements

Step 5: Create a One Value Motion Team

We recommend creating a small cross-functional team tasked with overseeing the integration of existing value management practices across the company. Ideally, the high-profile team will be situated within the office of the company's chief revenue officer, or even under the COO or CEO to provide the necessary authority to pull together the different departments behind the One Value Motion project. Staff the team with senior-level executives to ensure that the initiative's priorities align with the company's long-term strategic objectives. The One Value Motion team will need to define the scope of its work, roles, and responsibilities and determine how it will oversee and integrate existing value management programs.

To bring this idea to life, let's look at a hypothetical company looking to unify its customer-facing value management efforts (such as customer value discovery workshops, customer value assessments, and marketing case studies) that were being led by respective functional teams (value engineering, sales, and marketing). The One Value Motion team was created to bring all the horizontal shared services under its wing, unifying all customer value operations throughout the company (see Figure 9.3).

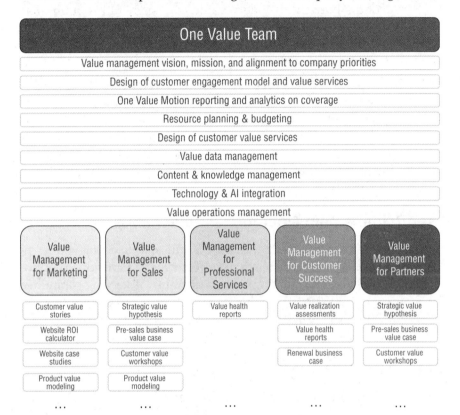

Figure 9.3: "One Value Motion" team charter example

Step 6: Secure the Budget

After executive management signs off on the initiative, the next step is to secure the budget for One Value Motion. The budget will have several core components:

Headcount   Estimating the size of the team will largely depend on the scope of work outlined in the previous steps. Best practice is to staff the team with diverse skill sets such as value engineers, CSMs, professional services team members, and project managers.

Technology   The One Value Motion team is ideally positioned to guide the deployment of value management technologies and tools, including AI. These tools—such as marketing and CRM systems—may be co-owned with other organizations, but the ability to customize or augment them will be essential to the success of the initiative. Modern value management programs also include leading value engineering platforms that automate and scale business cases, create lead-gen calculators, and measure customer value realization.

Program Spend   Some programs may need outside consulting services to develop value-focused methodologies, craft compelling value messages, deliver customer business cases, or conduct benchmark research. As you grow your program, these specialized resources can fill skill gaps including creative services (for sales asset creation), value modeling, business case consulting, and technical writing.

Step 7: Implement Operational Governance

Establishing strong program governance is critical to ensuring your company's One Value Motion is managed effectively and improved continuously. We recommend creating both an operational steering committee (to sponsor day-to-day VM activities) and an executive-level steering committee (to provide strategic guidance and budget approval)—both are good vehicles for proactively identifying and addressing program gaps and troubleshooting issues. Let's explore the typical roles and responsibilities of these governing committees.

Operational Steering Committee Charter

- Ensure that value management strategies are effectively implemented across all relevant business functions and share performance reports with executive steering committee.

- Coordinate the rollout and adoption of value management processes, tools, and best practices across all functional teams.

- Track key operational performance indicators (operational KPIs) related to value management, such as customer satisfaction, process adoption, customer activity levels, and operational success stories to promote the program overall.

- Identify and address operational challenges or bottlenecks in adopting value management processes and drive a continuous improvement program.

- Coordinate training and communication efforts to ensure all teams are aligned with the value management framework.

- Manage the allocation of One Value Motion resources (people, tools, budgets) needed to run value management programs.

Executive Steering Committee Charter

- Provide strategic direction for the value management initiative (One Value Motion), ensuring alignment with the company's long-term strategic objectives and communicate impact on to the CEO and board.

- Set governance policies and oversee AI compliance to ensure practices adhere to industry regulatory requirements and standards.

- Review and approve major investment decisions to support the company's value management strategy.

- Review the performance of One Value Motion against key strategic business performance metrics (pipeline growth, customer retention, value realization).

- Hold the Operational Steering Committee accountable for meeting One Value Motion's strategic objectives and expected outcomes.

- Continually improve the program's strategic direction, incorporating lessons learned and emerging best practices.

- Ensure that One Value Motion evolves in response to changes in the business environment and market conditions.

Step 8: Define One Value Motion Workflows

Once you create a solid governance structure and establish an operational budget, the first task is to map your customer's journey as a One Value Motion, identifying key touchpoints where value management practices can be added or enhanced. Figure 9.4 illustrates an example of a One Value Motion customer journey map showing all the relevant business functions and the critical activities performed at each point in the customer life cycle.

Awareness Phase

This is when product marketers build the solution's value model—including a *solution value tree*—highlighting key value drivers, algorithms (to measure business performance), and benchmarks. The *account-based marketing* team then translates this value model into marketing assets such as industry value reports (to prove out industry use cases), industry benchmarks, and customer success stories to drive value-based messaging to potential customers.

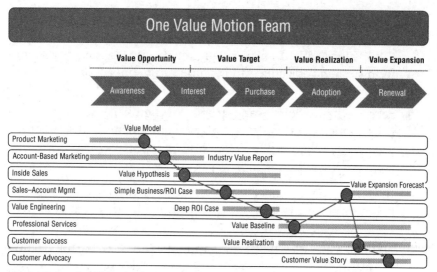

Figure 9.4:   One Value Motion journey map

Interest Phase

In this phase, *inside sales teams* design value-based tools to standardize and optimize the pre-sales "talk track" and pique interest in the solution. The goal is to identify high-potential prospects that can be passed to outside sales teams based on interest level and proclivity to purchase. After qualified leads are shared with the sales teams, it signals that the customer is ready to investigate the solution's value potential. This is when sales teams, partnering with the value engineering team as needed, can use AI-VM tools to build a simple business case (or sometimes a more detailed ROI analysis), which presents the expected business value outcomes for that specific customer.

Purchase Phase

As part of the One Value Motion workflow, you'll need to ensure that the product and services described (modeled) in the original business case aligns with what is eventually purchased. To do that, we recommend preparing a *Value Baseline Report* (usually drafted by the professional services or implementation team) that updates the scope and timing of the investment project to take into account any revisions that occurred during the procurement process. This step is essential for many large, multiyear investment projects because the timing and magnitude of the business KPIs can shift significantly because of these changes at the close of a deal.

Adoption and Renewal Phase

One Value Motion is designed to make sure the customer successfully adopts your solution and achieves the business outcomes it was promised, increasing the likelihood of contract renewal. To move confidently from adoption to renewal, it's essential that sales and customer success organizations work in tandem and communicate frequently. Too often, we've seen poor coordination between the groups result in cancelled renewals that could have been saved by proactive outreach by customer success teams.

In Figure 9.4, we highlight two activities that should begin immediately after the purchase is secured: Customer success teams should start value realization efforts to get ahead of any communication, change management, and performance measurement challenges that may arise during implementation, while sales teams should begin educating the customer on recommended next steps in its journey, providing road maps to unlock more value by building on the current purchase with complementary solutions.

Step 9: Design, Develop, and Deploy the AI Value Assistant

Having launched One Value Motion, it's time to leverage the unifying force that will make it truly scalable: an *AI-based value assistant*. This is an advanced conversational tool leveraging agentic AI capabilities[1] that integrates seamlessly with popular enterprise systems, including CRM, enterprise resource planning (ERP), marketing automation, value engineering, and content management platforms. Most enterprise B2B companies already possess many of these systems and manage vast amounts of value-oriented data that can be used to "train" the AI assistant. As a result, the AI value assistant can unlock and activate value intelligence to teams across the entire company.

---

[1] Agentic AI refers to a type of artificial intelligence (AI) that operates autonomously, making decisions, planning actions, and adapting to changing circumstances, similar to a human employee.

Drawing on these vast data resources, the AI value assistant can provide answers to any questions your teams may have about customer business value.

Your One Value Motion team will be responsible for developing and training the AI value assistant, integrating your company's unique business workflows with the value management workflows defined by the initiative. When done correctly, the assistant will revolutionize how your go-to-market teams operate by delivering detailed value intelligence, automating core One Value Motion tasks, and empowering functional teams to engage in more effective value conversations, ultimately enhancing pipeline growth and increasing win rates, renewals, and expansions.

The AI Value Assistant: Customer Insights at Your Fingertips

Value management practices enable go-to-market teams to engage in powerful value-based conversations with customers and partners—discussions that go well beyond just product features and functions. The AI value assistant will play a crucial role in enhancing these conversations, giving teams fast access to insights and recommendations informed by the company's enterprise systems and industry databases—and doing so without relying on the company's limited value engineering resources.

As the AI value assistant interacts with more users and gathers feedback from more customers, it becomes better at anticipating the types of questions teams might ask and the kinds of insights they find most valuable. This evolving capability will make the AI assistant an indispensable tool in value management, ensuring that teams are always equipped with the latest and most relevant information. Armed with value-based talking points, accurate business cases, and compelling forecasts of business outcomes, teams will gain the confidence to engage with customer decision-makers in powerful new ways.

VM PRO TIP

A human-like conversational interface is a key feature of most AI systems today. In the case of the AI value assistant, it acts as a knowledgeable companion that can be queried in natural language. For instance, a sales representative could ask, "What are the top three value drivers for this client?" or "How does our product's ROI compare to our competitors for this specific customer segment?" The AI assistant, drawing from integrated data sources across CRM, value engineering, ERP, and other systems, can instantly provide accurate and contextually relevant answers. This real-time access to insights not only saves time but also equips customer-facing teams with the information they need to tailor their conversations to the specific needs and concerns of each customer.

SALES CALLS WITH AN AI ASSISTANT BY YOUR SIDE

Imagine account executives, with a trusty AI value assistant by their side, quickly pulling up historical data on how similar customers have achieved positive ROI through the company's offerings. The assistant would suggest specific value propositions tailored to the customer's industry, size, and specific business pain points. With this timely information at their fingertips, sales reps can engage in more meaningful deal conversations that closely align with the customer's business objectives.

The Autonomous Worker: Powered by Agentic AI

In the past few years, the world has seen massive leaps in AI capabilities, with a steady march toward *agentic AI*—systems that can autonomously execute tasks across integrated systems. This capability is particularly valuable for value management programs, where timely and precise actions can have a big impact on the business, helping drive pipeline growth, win rates, renewals, and expansions. Although not extensively deployed in most operations today, we foresee that in the not-too-distant future—perhaps by the time this book is published—we will see agentic AI systems in a growing number of B2B enterprises.

COMING SOON: THE AUTONOMOUS LEAD MANAGEMENT ASSISTANT

Agentic AI systems have the potential to radically transform the lead-generation role. For example, after identifying a high-value prospect based on predictive analytics, the AI assistant will automatically trigger a series of actions, including:

- Scheduling a follow-up meeting with the prospect

- Drafting a personalized proposal based on the notes from the initial meeting

- Updating the CRM with relevant prospect deal insights

Similarly, in the case of customer renewals, the assistant could proactively trigger events such as:

- Identifying at-risk customer accounts

- Designing a tailored retention campaign through the marketing automation platform

- Notifying the customer success team to reach out with an automated and personalized value realization report

By automating routine yet essential value management actions, the AI value assistant—powered by agentic AI—will allow enterprise teams to focus on higher-value activities, such as nurturing customer relationships and crafting new strategic value propositions. Moreover, the assistant's ability to orchestrate actions across multiple information systems ensures that all elements of the value management process stay aligned and working in unison, thereby maximizing the potential for successful customer outcomes.

The AI Value Coach: Navigating Conversations in Real Time

Another example of how the AI value assistant will help teams navigate complex value discussions is by offering them real-time value coaching and customer engagement advice. For example, if a customer raises an objection or expresses uncertainty, the assistant will instantaneously provide the sales rep with detailed, data-supported counterarguments, or suggest alternative value propositions to convince the customer that the company can address their concerns. This dynamic, real-time support by the AI value assistant gives go-to-market teams confidence to steer customer conversations toward favorable outcomes, increasing the likelihood of closing deals and securing renewals or expansions.

VM PRO TIP

By handling routine tasks such as scheduling meetings and updating customer tracking systems, AI value assistants can enable a small number of value engineers to cover a much larger set of customers and deal opportunities, freeing up these valuable resources to focus on the largest and most complex customer deals.

The combined power of fast value insights, autonomous agentic actions, and real-time coaching will enhance your value conversations with customers, enabling your go-to-market teams to operate with greater precision and effectiveness.

Building Your AI Value Assistant

What's the best way to bring your AI value assistant to life? In this section, we'll talk about a couple ways to go about it and then describe a step-by-step process for developing an effective assistant to supercharge and scale your sales, marketing, and customer success teams.

We advise starting by creating an end-to-end customer value journey map (see Step 8 above), including a set of *value workflows* to give teams clarity around activities, roles, assets, and KPIs related to One Value Motion and serve as the blueprint for the design of the AI value assistant. Once these workflows are mapped, your AI designers can identify and prioritize top use cases for AI automation.

One of the early mistakes that enterprise AI adopters make is to view AI as a "jack of all trades" where companies implement AI tools (such as ChatGPT) and simply hope that they can be employed in some useful way, somewhere in the organization. This is an approach we call "spray and pray," and we believe it underutilizes the full potential of AI. It's a forgivable mistake because AI chatbots are easy to set up and fun to play with, and they help employees explore AI's potential impact on the business.

But while it offers AI-enabled content generation and summarization, this random approach may be harder to translate into financial benefit. Although the use of extensive prompt engineering, *retrieval augmented generation* (RAG), and predictive AI techniques can help solve specific problems fairly efficiently, achieving enterprise-scale business productivity can still prove elusive.

LARGE REASONING MODELS (LRMs): THE LATEST EVOLUTION IN AI TECHNOLOGY

The world of AI continues to march forward at a rapid pace. New AI models, techniques, and tools are being launched that will solve increasingly complex business challenges. And while the aim of this book is not to provide a deep exploration of the latest advancements in AI technology, we felt compelled to include a short introduction to a recent breakthrough that directly impacts our thesis of AI's impact on value management—namely, large reasoning models, or LRMs.

Also known as "reasoning AI," LRMs have the ability to process and interpret vast amounts of data to deliver highly logical, contextual, and sophisticated business insights. LRMs can understand complex human queries, analyze data trends, and generate intelligent recommendations. As a result, LRMs can be a highly relevant addition to your value management practice.

What is the difference between large language models (LLMs) and LRMs? While LLMs excel at processing and generating human-like text-based responses from language patterns, LRMs go well beyond this. LRMs can not only understand language patterns but also interpret logical relationships, draw inferences, and solve multistep problems that require deep analytical reasoning.

When combined, the capabilities of LLMs and LRMs become even more powerful. For example, LLMs can handle the natural language interactions between customers and stakeholders—generating responses and content—while LRMs can drive the underlying decision-making and problem-solving processes. Together, they enable enterprises to automate complex business workflows, providing intelligent communication and robust, data-driven reasoning for critical business functions like value management. LRMs can automate value management activities such as analyzing and extracting key customer insights, evaluating customer performance data, and recommending strategies to optimize customer engagement.

Here's a quick comparison of LLMs and LRMs:

VALUE MANAGEMENT CAPABILITIES (EXAMPLES)	LLM	LRM
Understand/generate natural language	Y	Y
Analyze customer interactions and feedback	Y	Y
Process and reason with structured data	N	Y
Generate business value reports	Limited	Y
Provide insights for customer engagement strategies	Y	Y

VALUE MANAGEMENT CAPABILITIES (EXAMPLES)	LLM	LRM
Automate multistep decision-making	N	Y
Optimize resource allocation based on value impact	N	Y
Identify patterns in customer behavior	Y	Y
Perform logical reasoning and inference	N	Y
Drive personalized recommendations for upsell/cross-sell opportunities	Limited	Y

In short, LRMs offer a massive opportunity for companies to revolutionize how enterprises orchestrate customer-facing functions to achieve value management at scale. Be sure to leverage the power of reasoning AI the next time you craft "to-be" use cases for your AI-driven value management projects.

Targeted Workflow AI Assistant Approach

We recommend taking a more targeted, workflow-integration approach to deploying AI tools. This involves using custom-built AI value assistant applications that are integrated with other enterprise applications to create a *digitized workflow*. Since these targeted AI value tools are engineered to work within existing business workflows, it's easier to drive productivity and speed user adoption. The idea is to deploy AI value tools to automate manual tasks without disrupting the conventional work processes that people are already familiar with. Some selected workflows could be radically redesigned or even fully automated with AI, and these opportunities should be pursued to maximize the impact of the tools.

VM PRO TIP

AI assistants serve as a copilot to your value management teams by answering key questions like "What solutions have the customer deployed, and to what level of maturity?" or "What are the top three value drivers for a solution?" While AI copilots provide significant value, human consultants still need to manage and coordinate the creation of key deliverables like business cases. But what if AI could handle the entire workflow? That's where agentic AI comes into play.

Agentic AI automates and orchestrates workflows such as business case development or preparing for a customer quarterly business review (QBR).

It builds on foundational AI models that include key features like function calling, retrieval augmented generation (RAG), and code interpreter, making it possible for AI to manage tasks like customer value discovery, business case creation, and research.

- **Function calling** retrieves real-time data or generates reports from external systems and APIs.

- **RAG** pulls relevant and up-to-date information from internal or external sources to ensure contextually accurate insights.

- **Code interpreters** run calculations and data analysis, providing visualizations for tasks like financial projections and ROI analysis.

By integrating these capabilities, agentic AI enables intelligent value management workflows that automate data gathering, analysis, and task execution, freeing value management consultants to focus on strategy and client engagement.

When designing an AI value management workflow, automation should streamline repetitive tasks, while ensuring human oversight for critical decision-making. Each workflow should be customizable for specific business actions, with AI handling data-intensive tasks and humans refining outputs to meet project goals.

For example, when creating a business case, the consultant defines the scope and financial targets. The AI uses function calling to pull financial benchmarks, RAG to gather case studies, and a code interpreter to run ROI calculations and generate data visualizations. The consultant then reviews the AI-generated content, adjusts projections, and ensures alignment with the client's financial goals before finalizing the business case.

Phase 1: Discovery and Planning

During this early phase of developing an AI toolset, you engage stakeholders, identify and prioritize use cases, gather requirements, conduct feasibility analyses, and design the technical solution architecture.

Engage Stakeholders

Engaging company stakeholders will help develop a detailed understanding of the business needs, goals, and key challenges that need to be addressed by the AI value assistant. Primarily this involves collecting input directly from AI user groups with the help of workshops and interviews with key stakeholders across sales, marketing, customer success, and partner organizations. The goal is to uncover current pain points, AI system requirements, and business outcome expectations for the AI value assistant solution. To help create interview guides for these sessions, you can find examples of challenges and use cases in the earlier chapters of this book.

AI GUARDRAIL #1: IDENTIFY EMPLOYEE CONCERNS

During stakeholder engagement sessions, be sure to include discussions around data privacy, corporate ethics, and industry compliance to help identify any employee concerns, or specific corporate regulations that must be adhered to.

Identify and Prioritize Use Cases

Next, create a prioritized set of business use cases to support the initial release of your AI value assistant. These can include business case creation, customer and deal research summarization, buyer journey handoff support, and marketing and sales KPI reporting assistance. The AI value assistant design team should assess the business use cases based on financial impact, operational feasibility, competitive urgency, and alignment with strategic business goals.

AI GUARDRAIL #2: INCORPORATE ETHICAL CONSIDERATIONS

As you evaluate business use cases for your AI value assistant, seriously consider any ethical implications. For example, some AI tools can be applied in ways that may impact the privacy of your employees. Before launching the assistant, designers should prioritize use cases that do not include datasets that could breach your company's ethical standards.

Table 9.3 presents a comprehensive set of AI functional business use cases that we detailed in the earlier chapters of this book.

Table 9.3: Comprehensive AI business use cases

#	FUNCTIONAL AREA	AI-VM USE CASE
1	Marketing	Autogenerate drafts of value propositions and competitive positioning analyses.
2	Marketing	Generate reports using value intelligence and competitive pricing insights.

Continues

Table 9.3: (*continued*)

#	FUNCTIONAL AREA	AI-VM USE CASE
3	Marketing	Create value intelligence content for various channels and customer journey stages.
4	Marketing	Develop customer reference stories based on value intelligence.
5	Marketing	Generate ideal customer profile (ICP) lists using CRM data and social media interactions.
6	Marketing	Draft value-based whitepapers based on reference stories and market research.
7	Marketing	Produce co-branded marketing assets that reflect joint-value propositions with partners.
8	Marketing	Recommend value propositions based on new product and customer developments.
9	Sales	Analyze target's solution usage to predict value opportunities and recommend positioning.
10	Sales	Provide recommendations on marketing and sales tactics, including prospect nurturing and messaging.
11	Sales	Offer conversational support for prospects researching solutions.
12	Sales	Generate reports on event discussions, bookings, and engagement recommendations.
13	Sales	Recommend event sessions, booth activities, and networking opportunities to participants.
14	Sales	Assist in rapid solution pilot setup by matching profiles with previous customer experiences.
15	Sales	Design implementation plans using insights from multiple deployment teams.
16	Sales	Enhance sales and pipeline forecast accuracy with predictive AI.
17	Sales	Automate pipeline management and provide real-time sales opportunity visibility.
18	Sales	Tailor training programs for sales reps based on performance analysis.
19	Sales	Provide real-time answers to queries about deals requiring value management support.

#	FUNCTIONAL AREA	AI-VM USE CASE
20	Professional Services	Transcribe meetings and structure notes into templates focused on business objectives and solutions.
21	Professional Services	Structure value assessment results into templates covering ROI and strategic benefits.
22	Customer Success	Summarize customer success data and generate business outcomes realization reports.
23	Customer Success	Consult on value-related questions and recommend tailored solutions during events.
24	Customer Success	Review product data and customer success metrics to determine realized value and suggest opportunities.
25	Customer Success	Facilitate cross-language collaboration by translating documents and outputs.
26	Partners	Assist partners in developing value-based marketing strategies and creating co-branded assets.
27	Partners	Provide custom-fit value proposition recommendations for specific customer deals.
28	Partners	Help partners identify industry use cases supported by joint solutions and recommend go-to-market strategies.
29	Partners	Summarize project materials and generate business outcomes reports with recommendations for further value.
30	Professional Services	Automatically generate drafts of final presentation deliverables.
31	Sales	Automate routine tasks in digitized workflows, allowing focus on high-value activities.
32	Sales	Analyze historical sales data and market trends to improve sales and pipeline forecasts.
33	Sales	Generate real-time reports to ensure accurate and timely reporting.
34	Sales	Automate notifications when new sales opportunities arise.
35	Sales	Forecast and measure individual KPIs and metrics for value management consultants and sellers.
36	Sales	Analyze performance and create interactive training modules for on-demand learning.

Continues

Table 9.3: (*continued*)

#	FUNCTIONAL AREA	AI-VM USE CASE
37	Sales	Provide real-time database query answers about new deals requiring value management support.
38	Sales	Perform sentiment analysis on emails and CRM notes for customer insights.
39	Customer Success	Assist with account planning and business case development through industry and company research.
40	Sales	Automate engagement creation based on deal or account variables.
41	Partners	Optimize joint-sales opportunities by using value management content from partner systems.

Gather Requirements

With your business use cases prioritized, the next step is to collaborate with stakeholders to define their functional and technical requirements. Be sure to drill down into each use case to develop a complete understanding of your current and future workflows, enabled by AI. This can involve developing user stories, acceptance criteria, and technical specifications for each business use case.

AI GUARDRAIL #3: DOCUMENT DATA USAGE

As part of requirements gathering, be sure to extensively document specific data usage requirements. This will be essential to ensure compliance with rules and regulations related to data privacy (data anonymization), ethical AI usage (bias mitigation), and other corporate, industry, and government compliance mandates (such as the European Union's General Data Protection Regulation [GDPR] and the California Consumer Privacy Act [CCPA]).

Conduct Feasibility Analysis

Conduct a study to evaluate the technical and operational feasibility of implementing your AI value assistant. This is important because the technical features needed to deploy AI-VM use cases can vary across multiple technology platforms. The feasibility study should cover requirements for operational resources, toolsets, and infrastructure technologies required, along with any potential operational and technical risks and mitigation strategies needed in the event of a data breach, technical problem, or system outage.

AI GUARDRAIL #4: MINIMIZE PRIVACY RISK

When developing a feasibility study, be sure to address potential ethical and privacy risks posed by the AI assistant's operational and technical specifications. Track and control who has access to the information shared by the assistant with an eye to preventing the unauthorized sharing of confidential information.

Design a Technical Solution Architecture

With the overall feasibility of the system verified, the next step is to design the technical architecture of the AI value assistant, including integration points with your existing business systems. This is a critical step toward unifying the existing value management workstreams into a holistic One Value Motion program.

AI GUARDRAIL #5: ENFORCE TRANSPARENCY AND ACCOUNTABILITY

As part of your AI value assistant, build intelligent AI practices such as transparency and accountability into the architecture design. For example, make sure employees only have access to customer and deal data from their region unless otherwise approved by your legal and finance organization.

Phase 2: Design and Development

At this point in your AI value toolset development, you're ready to finalize your data strategy, design and train the AI model, and design the AI value assistant.

Data Strategy and Integration

Now that the technical architecture has been finalized, the next step is to define your solution's data strategy, which should specify data sources, data models, and data integration points across existing corporate systems. The effort will deliver:

- Data integration plans
- Extract, transform, and load (ETL) process maps
- Data flow diagrams
- Data mapping documentation

AI GUARDRAIL #6: CONDUCT COMPLIANCE REVIEWS

Include in your data strategy a review of your data compliance and protection regulations and recommendations, such as data minimization, encryption, secure data storage.

AI Model Design and Training

Few B2B companies today build their own proprietary LLMs, but instead rely on foundation models readily available from the likes of OpenAI and Google. Your company can license these models to develop enterprise-specific AI applications for a wide range of uses, and you can configure the models to address individual business processes, cultural differences, and data sources. In this step, AI designers collect and preprocess company data to train the AI model that powers your AI value toolset.

User Interface and Experience (UI/UX) Design

With the underlying model complete, the design team can now focus on the front-end user experience. This effort includes the design of user interface (UI) wireframes and mockups, and a finalized UI/UX workflow that aligns with your user needs and preferences. The design of the user interface for the AI value toolset must be intuitive and user-friendly, ensuring adoption by value management teams across all business functions.

Development of the AI Toolset

Now with the front- and back-end designs complete, we are ready to build the AI value toolset. In this step, the design team builds the solution's conversational interface, integrating the interface with the trained AI models, and connecting the AI value toolset to existing enterprise IT systems.

AI GUARDRAIL #7: ENFORCE SECURE CODING PRACTICES

During AI value assistant development, be sure to enforce secure development coding practices and implement technical features that protect user privacy such as data anonymization and access controls. Ensure also that these capabilities address any AI value assistant ethical guideline requirements.

Phase 3: Testing and Validation

Before deploying the AI value assistant, you'll need to test and validate the solution, including unit testing, user acceptance testing, and performance and security testing.

Unit and Integration Testing

This step ensures that the individual components of the system are performing properly. In fact, the success of the AI value assistant will largely hinge on the various functional units performing as designed, so *unit testing* is particularly important. Also, integration testing should be performed to ensure that the assistant works seamlessly with existing software systems and doesn't create any performance issues across the IT environment.

AI GUARDRAIL #8: TEST THE RIGHT THINGS

Include unit testing that validates the data privacy and security handling within the AI value assistant solution. Ethical testing should be layered into the unit tests to ensure the AI models are providing fair and unbiased results.

User Acceptance Testing

AI is a new technology for users and solution designers, so pay special attention to user acceptance testing (UAT). If you embed the AI value assistant directly into business workflows (our recommended strategy), UAT can help ensure proper execution and use adoption before cutting over to live production. By engaging users across multiple business groups, you give employees the opportunity to test the solution in real-world scenarios.

AI GUARDRAIL #9: THWART BAD ACTORS

During UAT, incorporate user testing that specifically addresses potential concerns related to privacy, transparency, and ethical behavior of the AI solution. It is important to gather this feedback before the system goes live.

Performance and Security Testing

The final task in this step is performance and security testing, which ensures the AI value assistant can manage a range of workloads without compromising the user experience while protecting sensitive data from being hacked by bad actors both inside and outside the company.

AI GUARDRAIL #10: DOCUMENT CYBERSECURITY REQUIREMENTS

Conducting rigorous cybersecurity testing to protect against data breaches and unauthorized access is critical to the success of the AI value assistant. Be sure to document your system's security and privacy requirements in collaboration with relevant C-suite executives such as the chief information security officer (CISO) and the board of directors' Risk and Compliance Committee.

Phase 4: Deployment and Adoption

The time has come to launch your AI value assistant. Here's how to do it.

Deployment Planning

With testing complete, your AI value assistant is ready to deploy. To ensure a successful launch, you'll want to develop a detailed deployment plan that includes a project timeline, resource allocation, and a rollback strategy if any problems arise.

Pilot Deployment

Given the strategic importance of the AI value assistant, it's a good idea to pilot the solution before you launch it companywide. Start with a small group of users in each department to monitor the solution's performance, gather feedback, and tune the AI assistant to ensure success when you are ready for full deployment.

Full-Scale Deployment

Companywide deployment of the AI value assistant will take a lot more than a flip of a switch. Given the solution's significant impact across the enterprise, a full-scale deployment will require investments in user training and change management, technical tuning to ensure maximum system performance, and ongoing monitoring of user adoption, business productivity, and program effectiveness. These efforts will include activities and assets such as:

- Launch communications
- User help guides
- User training and coaching programs
- Executive management launch performance dashboards

Phase 5: Post-Deployment Support and Continuous Improvement

There's more work to be done after the launch of your AI value assistant.

Continuous Improvement

AI solution's inherent self-learning ML capabilities will help the solution perform better over time. But a lot of the improvements will come from the monitoring, support, and feedback mechanisms your design team puts in place to create a continuous improvement program for the solution. This should include establishing an AI support team to address any issues that arise and gather ongoing feedback from the user community to spot opportunities for future improvement.

Reporting and Value Realization

Finally, we recommend developing relevant business success metrics to track and document ongoing program performance and value realization. Create a convenient performance dashboard to give executive sponsors line of sight into the AI value assistant's positive business impact. The solution will likely take some time to get up to speed, so don't expect dramatic results right away. That's why tracking program performance over time will be critical for guiding future investment and resource decisions. Key business metrics to track should include core sales metrics such as pipeline growth, win rates, renewals, and customer share-of-wallet expansion.

Reaping the Rewards of One Value Motion

We believe that when you take the crucial next step of establishing a unified One Value Motion program encompassing the entire enterprise—augmented by a next-generation AI value assistant—you will unlock the power of AI-drive value management on a massive scale. But how much can you expect to gain from a comprehensive AI-VM program over time? In Chapter 10, "Delivering Business Outcomes with AI-Powered Value Management," we'll put pen to paper and estimate a range of likely business outcomes, from significantly greater sales revenue and more productive marketing to customer loyalty and growth.

Delivering Business Outcomes with AI-Powered Value Management

In Chapter 9, "One Value Motion: The Power of Unified Value Management," we laid out a powerful approach that will help companies scale their value management programs by adopting a unified, AI-enabled, value management framework connecting the entire enterprise. We saw how this holistic approach—One Value Motion—can drive efficiencies by integrating value management into each phase of the customer life cycle to deliver exponentially greater financial outcomes for a business.

With AI solutions, including the AI value assistant described in Chapter 9, companies can solve the problem of scale, enabling them to automate time-consuming tasks, accelerate value-based content creation, and streamline collaboration across functional teams. Costs are contained because AI systems can significantly reduce the need for high-priced value engineers, consultants, and other resources that would have been needed to expand VM programs.

How much more value can B2B companies expect to realize by adopting AI-driven value management approaches? In this chapter, we'll put pen to paper and estimate a range of likely business outcomes, such as revenue growth, accelerated sales cycles, and customer loyalty. As much as possible, we'll aim to quantify these outcomes in business performance metrics that matter to B2B enterprises, including lead-generation rates, deal win rates, and customer churn.

Let's start with AI-VM's impact on the top line.

Boosting Revenue Throughout the Customer Life Cycle

Earlier in the book, we showed how the combination of VM practices and AI tools can accelerate sales and lift revenue throughout the customer life cycle. We identified three primary drivers:

- **Increased lead generation:** By more effectively targeting and engaging prospects with AI-VM strategies and tools, companies can convert potential buyers to sales-qualified leads/prospects at double the average rate or greater, setting the stage for rising sales.

- **Improved deal win rate:** These same AI-VM programs, which help customers understand the expected business value of a proposed B2B solution, can increase their propensity to buy and lead to 2X higher deal win rates.

- **Better customer retention, contract renewals and upsells:** When companies use AI-VM to track customer performance and automatically share business improvements, it increases the likelihood that customers will renew and expand their contract (and not defect) by a factor of 2X or more.

Added together, these AI-VM-driven improvements can be a significant driver of revenue growth. Simply put, by doubling the sales opportunities (from improving marketing's ability to generate sales qualified leads) and then doubling a company's sales win rates, companies end up closing four times more deals compared to their pre-AI-VM baseline. This translates into a customer base that's four times larger and could help companies retain even more revenue at the end of the product's life cycle or when their customer contracts (enterprise license agreements) come up for renewal (typically 3–5 years out). As mentioned in Chapter 8, "AI-Driven Value Management for Customer Success," companies can boost customer retention by equipping their customer success teams with AI-VM tools and strategies that can effectively reduce customer churn.

Of course, the magnitude of retained revenue from improved customer success activities will depend on the starting point—namely, their previous churn rate. The higher a company's legacy churn rate, the greater the revenue boost from implementing VM-based customer success activities that demonstrate value realized by a product or service. To illustrate this relationship, we've created an AI-VM customer retention impact sensitivity table that shows the magnitude of benefit across a spectrum of legacy churn rates (see Figure 10.1).

Customer Retention Impact

Legacy Churn Rate	AI-VM Churn Rate	Churn Rate Improvement	Customer Retention Improvement
80%	40%	40%	200%
70%	35%	35%	117%
60%	30%	30%	75%
50%	25%	25%	50%
40%	20%	20%	33%
30%	15%	15%	22%
20%	10%	10%	13%
10%	5%	5%	5%

Figure 10.1: AI-VM-based customer retention impact

As you can see, AI-VM-based customer success solutions can deliver increasingly greater benefits for companies that have higher churn rates. Note that there are a few nuances regarding how and when these customer success business outcomes are achieved. First, since the effect of retaining more customers will only be realized at the end of a subscription or a product life cycle, its impact will be staggered over time. Second, AI-VM programs in customer success organizations generate an accumulating annual impact because it allows companies to retain an increasing percentage of the new customers captured by AI-VM's marketing and sales activities. This drives an exponential increase in customer expansion and positive business outcomes for these AI-VM programs over time.

How AI-VM Can Drive Revenue: A 10-Year Forecast

Now let's estimate how AI-VM programs could help companies boost revenue over a 10-year period. In this scenario, let's assume that the company has a three-year product license contract (enterprise license agreement [ELA]) and historically has lost about 10 percent of its customer base each year (legacy churn rate).

Fast-forward: The company launches several new AI-driven value management programs, which generate more customer leads and close more deals every year. As a result, the company successfully acquires about four times more customers over the first three years of the contract. By year 4, the first group of (incremental) new customers is now due for renewal.

But thanks to efforts of its customer success team, augmented by AI-VM tools and tactics, the company will see an additional bump to its revenue stream. That's because it has now reduced customer churn to 5 percent, or half of its former churn rate, translating into a 4 percent additional lift to its customer base on top of the 400 percent growth in customers by year 4 (see Figure 10.2). By lowering its churn rate, the company continues to enlarge its customer base each year as its "installed base" builds on itself. By year 10, the incremental impact of improved customer retention adds 26 percent to the 400 percent revenue lift. Note that if the company had started with an even higher churn rate, it would likely accrue even more incremental revenue than this scenario presents.

	YR 1	YR 2	YR 3	Yr 4	YR 5	YR 6	YR 7	YR 8	YR 9	YR 10
Traditional	1	2	3	5	8	11	17	25	36	52
AI-VM	4	8	12	20	31	47	70	103	152	222
% Increase	400%	400%	400%	404%	408%	411%	414%	418%	422%	426%

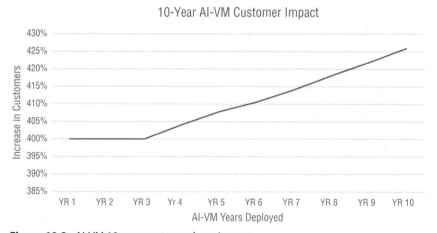

Figure 10.2: AI-VM 10-year customer base impact

REAPING REWARDS FROM AI-VM: A HYPOTHETICAL CASE STUDY

Let's add some color to this scenario and see how the introduction of AI-VM programs might play out at a fictional company we'll call Acme Manufacturing Corp. With customers worldwide, Acme fields a large sales-force that closes more than a thousand deals per year from traditional sales operations. After integrating AI-driven value management into its operations, the company is now reaping the rewards across marketing, sales, and customer success to generate a 4X improvement in customer acquisition. It also cut its churn rate in half, from 10 percent to 5 percent.

More Productive Marketing

For years, Acme's marketing team had been following a traditional "wide funnel" approach to gathering sales leads. Considered one of the best marketers in the industry, the company was paying top dollar to identify prospects through paid lists and digital advertising. The marketing group had become comfortable with identifying about 100,000 potential leads each year and only turning about 6 percent of them into credible prospects—on par with the industry average.

The broad strategy was costly, though, prompting the company to embrace new AI-VM approaches that combined value-based messaging with AI-driven account-based marketing digital campaigns. Soon, marketers found they could identify more leads from a smaller pool and target prospects with a higher likelihood of conversion. As a result, Acme cut its digital advertising spending in half and improved its conversion rate to 30 percent, moving from 6,000 sales qualified leads per year to 12,000 sales qualified leads—a 2X improvement.

Taking Sales to New Levels

Acme's sales organization was also considered a high performer, with a 20 percent close rate and an average time to close a deal of 2–3 months. But sales felt it could do more and decided to implement AI-VM sales programs that helped account teams reduce time-to-close even more. Much of the performance boost was due to an inflow of better qualified leads from the marketing group, which started using value intelligence strategies to clearly communicate the business impact of Acme's products to potential customers. This meant sales teams were starting from a jog instead of a walk and could "continue the conversation" with the customer by providing more detailed and quantifiable evidence of how Acme's products would improve the customer's specific business operations. The team's laser focus on business value—enhanced by AI-driven communications—ultimately led to a doubling of its average deal win rate.

Building on Customer Success

Acme had been doing a good job of keeping customers happy with its products and services, thanks largely to the energetic efforts of its customer success team, which helped keep churn rates at 10 percent—a historical low for the industry. But the company saw an opportunity for improvement by deploying AI-VM customer success practices and tools to strengthen its partnership with customers across their product life cycles. Indeed, the customer success team gradually transformed its role from a ticket-taking customer service department to a trusted partner committed to helping customers realize greater business value—for example, by formulating recommendations on how customers can deploy Acme's products in innovative and profitable new ways.

This new relationship enhanced Acme's revenue performance in two ways. First, it was able to retain twice as many customers each year. This was driven by its ability to demonstrate to customers, in hard numbers, the business outcomes they were achieving, making contract renewals that much easier. Second, Acme's success teams could tap AI-VM solutions to offer customers timely guidance on how and when to seize new opportunities using their existing and new products. The following graphic shows Acme's business outcomes: traditional vs. AI-VM strategies.

Sales Funnel Stage	Traditional	AI-VM
Awareness—Lead Generation	100,000 targeted leads 6% marketing conversion rate **6,000 SQLs**	40,000 targeted leads 30% marketing conversion rate **12,000 SQLs**
Interest to Decision—Sales Engagement	Deal close time: 2–3 months 20% sales win rate **1,200 Deals Closed**	Deal close time: 1–2 months 40% sales win rate **4,800 Deals Closed**
Renewal—Customer Success & Expansion	10% churn rate **1,080 Customers Retained**	5% churn rate **4,560 Customers Retained**

Capturing More Value from Your Partner Ecosystem

We've seen how AI-driven value management can produce outsized benefits for companies across every part of the business, leading to more productive lead generation, faster deal closings and win rates, and greater customer renewals. The resulting revenue boost clearly justifies serious investments in value-based marketing, sales, and customer success programs powered by AI technologies.

But there is more value to be had for B2B companies by extending AI-VM programs to support partner sales channels and ecosystems, which, as discussed in Chapter 7, "Empowering Your Sales Partners with AI-Driven Value Management," can account for 70–80 percent of the primary company's sales. However, despite providing valuable products and services to the end customer, many partners lack the budget and labor needed to run a successful value management program. B2B companies that ignore their partner channel and focus on just improving their own sales funnel can leave significant revenue opportunities on the table.

In fact, when channel partners adopt modern AI-driven value management tools and practices, they invariably experience the same positive business impacts enjoyed by their sponsoring company—namely, 2X lead generation, 2X close rates, and 2X retention rates. What's more, since small and mid-sized partners tend to trail behind industry leaders in deploying the latest marketing, sales, and customer success practices, the introduction of AI-VM strategies and tools can help them close this gap and lead to even more revenue opportunities compared to their larger sponsors.

That's good news for the sponsoring company, too, which benefits from a growing and more profitable partner ecosystem enabled by AI-VM. For example, let's say a company gets 50 percent of its sales through its partner channel and then adopts AI-VM channel partner practices that leads to a 4X sales results boost for its partners. That would translate into a doubling of sales results for the sponsoring company. For a company that earns 75 percent of its sales through the channel, the revenue impact would amount to up to 300 percent (see Figure 10.3). It's simple math, but exciting to see how it can add up for a company that manages a significant partner channel.

Channel Sales (as % of Total Sales)	AI-VM Impact
10%	11%
25%	33%
50%	100%
75%	300%
85%	567%

Figure 10.3: AI-VM channel sales revenue impact sensitivity

Driving Cost and Time Savings

Not only can well-designed AI-driven value management programs help expand a business's top line, but it can also rein in costs, enriching its bottom line. The reason is the inherent cost-effectiveness of AI, which enables companies to replicate and scale its value management programs—and the talent that runs them—across functional business groups. The AI value assistant becomes an important tool in keeping program costs down, especially as the programs extend across business groups.

Let's face it: High-powered value management teams aren't cheap. The typical value engineer can command salaries ranging from $200,000 to over $500,000 a year. And because they're in high demand, these resources can take months or more to hire and can be difficult to train and deploy. The goal of integrating AI into a value management program is to optimize and focus the efforts of these expert resources.

Using AI value assistants, companies can quickly scale their value engineering resources by harnessing their knowledge and techniques to meet the increasing value management needs of sales, marketing, and customer success teams, as well as those of partner communities. Meanwhile, that leaves the company's value management experts free to focus on higher-value tasks, such as creating compelling business-value content and helping close strategic customer deals.

We believe the primary role for value engineers is to focus their unique skill set to help their companies close their largest and most strategic deals and provide personalized "white glove" services for these customers' top executives. If more companies could learn to use AI value assistants to replicate just 80 percent of their value engineers' capabilities, we believe that would be a huge win for their businesses.

It's hard to estimate precisely the cost savings companies can acheive from deploying AI value assistants and digital twins in place of human value engineers. We can, however, estimate the potential labor cost savings by looking at current value management teams and modeling the potential efficiency gain from using AI for these resources. Let's assume that the typical value engineer today is responsible for a portfolio of activities, including:

- Developing value-based thought leadership content
- Formulating business cases in support of strategic accounts
- Creating lead-generation tools and top-of-funnel value messaging
- Supporting value-based solution sales tools and training
- Providing tools, training, and support for customer success teams (renewals)

As you can imagine, value engineering teams have a lot on their plates, and they're often juggling a lot of projects at once. Facing limited resources and tight budgets, the average value management team spends most of its time working with the sales organization to support high-profile deals and training sales teams how to use the ROI business case tools they create. This leaves value engineers precious little time to provide their value management expertise to other business functions such as marketing, partner sales, and customer success.

Once AI value assistants are deployed, we expect the various functional teams to need less hands-on support by value engineering team. This will allow value engineering teams to spend more time—we estimate as much as 3X more—focusing on developing and sharing value intelligence, performing thought leadership activities, and doubling-down on strategic customer accounts, as shown in Figure 10.4.

Activity	Legacy	AI-VM	Increase
Value Thought Leadership	10%	30%	3x
Strategic Account Business Cases	30%	60%	2x
Marketing Top-of-Funnel Support	10%	2%	
Sales Tools/VM-Training Support	40%	6%	
Customer Success/VM-Training Support	10%	2%	

Figure 10.4: Value engineering activities: percentage of capacity legacy vs. AI-VM enabled

So how does this translate into cost savings? By using AI to scale these high-value experts and focus them on activities yielding the highest returns, we believe value management programs will almost certainly become more productive—we estimate 5X more—enabling companies to support a One Value Motion AI-VM program with only one-fifth of the resources and cost. For example, if we take a large SaaS provider managing a team of 200 resources today, increasing the team's productivity by 80 percent could potentially save $56 million annually (see Figure 10.5).

SaaS VE Team Annual Cost Savings—Example

Average Annual Cost of a Value Engineer	$350,000
Size of VE Team	200
Annual VE Team FTE Cost	$70,000,000
AI-VM Productivity Impact	80%
Potential AI-VM Annual Cost Savings	$56,000,000

Figure 10.5: SaaS company AI-VM value engineering team productivity savings

Of course, these savings will likely be offset by costs associated with developing and maintaining the AI systems that power these productivity gains. In addition, successfully scaling value engineering teams to achieve this level of savings will hinge on the effectiveness of the AI tools being used by the various functional teams and partner organizations. However, the sheer magnitude of the productivity cost savings promises to provide a large cushion that would drive significant ROI from just a cost-savings perspective.

Looking forward, we expect AI-driven value management to become a transformative breakthrough for B2B companies of all sizes. We've projected a 4X revenue lift for companies that leverage AI-VM tools and technologies to double leads and deal win rates. Companies can then add to their revenue stream by using AI-VM to shrink churn rates, helping grow their customer base and retain more customers. As companies adopt value-based programs and seek to extend the practice to more parts of the business, AI solutions will help keep costs under control, using these emerging technologies to drive dramatic efficiency and productivity savings. We are excited to see how quickly these innovations ripple through the B2B economy and deliver on our expectations of exponentially greater business outcomes.

## CHAPTER 11

A Final Note to the Reader

With AI's rise, business norms are being disrupted, and value management is indeed one of the key beneficiaries of this transformation. What we have strived to do in this book is to offer you a blueprint—the strategy, tools, ideas, and end-to-end business frameworks—to take full advantage of AI's potential to build a world-class value management program.

In closing, it is worth reiterating some key messages from this book.

Value management isn't just about sales or business cases—it's about uniting the entire enterprise and its customer-facing functions around a common goal: customer value. As defined in this book, value management is the art and science of helping customers achieve exceptional business outcomes, which in turn drives pipeline growth, deal wins, and customer expansion for your company. This capability spans marketing, customer success, professional services, alliance partners, and more. The true power of value management is unlocked when integrated across the customer life cycle, supported by investments in people, processes, and technology. The real-world examples in this book show how each business function plays a strategic role in making that happen.

We explained how scaling value management to achieve significant revenue outcomes—doubling pipeline, deal wins, and expansion (what we've called "2-to-the-power-of-3 business outcomes")—requires a robust investment that is both costly and time-intensive. We then discussed how AI has the potential to change the game. The AI-enabled value management use cases presented throughout this book demonstrate how AI can scale these capabilities far beyond what was once imaginable, covering more customers, deals, and channel partners. The AI-VM blueprint presented in this book allows you to forecast, track, and report customer value at scale, achieving these business outcomes faster than ever. Now, companies can scale value management bigger, better, and faster—without spending the millions of dollars in investment required without AI.

However, we do not believe that AI alone is the silver bullet. The AI-VM blueprint must be implemented with strategic intent, integrated into well-defined business process workflows, and supported by strong leadership sponsorship. As you begin using AI in your value management program, you will need to modify the blueprint presented in this book to fit your organization's specific goals and needs. The AI technology platforms are ready to support AI-VM, but your challenge will lie in developing your own business use cases and then fine-tuning AI to become a productive partner for your go-to-market teams. The companies that build AI value assistants—designed to master their solutions, understand customer needs, and integrate value management across the enterprise—will emerge as the industry leaders.

Encourage your teams to experiment with AI but do so with a clear strategic vision. Align your leadership around AI as a transformative go-to-market approach, not just another toolset. Establish AI guardrails to address privacy, security, bias, and other concerns. It's also important to quantify and communicate the risk-adjusted return from AI-VM investments to top management.

Looking forward, it's important that we stay humble and realize that we're still in the early stages of AI technologies, requiring us to stay vigilant about new AI developments. The pace of AI innovation is staggering! This book has focused on proven value management fundamentals while also providing a framework for incorporating new AI capabilities as they emerge. Be prepared to not only adopt these AI advancements but also to rethink business process workflows and business models to fully harness AI's potential.

AI will continue to evolve, opening new doors to redefine value management in the B2B world. This book is just the starting point with which you can leapfrog to the front—and stay ahead of the game.

We hope you find this book serves as a useful tool to build a successful value management capability for your organization!

Glossary

A

account-based marketing (ABM)—A growth strategy where marketing and sales teams collaborate to target high-revenue potential accounts.

agentic AI—AI that autonomously makes decisions and adapts to changing conditions without human oversight.

AI-based value assistant/copilot—A chatbot that mimics a value management consultant's actions using AI technologies like predictive AI and generative AI. It can assist within a CRM or value automation tool, answering questions and performing tasks, or conduct entire workflows such as creating business cases.

AI-VM—AI-driven value management, where AI enhances the efficiency and accuracy of value management tasks.

B

business value assessment/customer value assessment—A formal business case outlining how a technology investment will help the customer meet goals like cost savings, productivity improvements, or revenue growth. Created in collaboration with the customer using provided data.

C

capital expenditures (CapEx) savings—Savings from reduced spending on long-term assets like property or machinery, which are considered business investments.

CRM platforms—Tools that help sales teams manage customer relationships and sales data, tracking opportunities and customer interactions. Examples include Salesforce, SAP, and Oracle.

customer executive briefings—Presentations for customer leadership, often by value teams, to showcase how solutions address industry or functional needs. These can include demos, business case discussions, and strategic talks.

customer success platforms—Tools that provide insights into customer retention and realized business outcomes, using value trees to collect relevant data, often from product telemetry.

customer success team—A post-sales team focused on improving customer satisfaction, adoption, and retention through services like integration support and value realization assessments.

cycle time improvement—Reducing the time it takes to complete a task or process to increase efficiency and productivity.

D

deal/opportunity—A potential sales transaction with a new or existing customer, including upsell or cross-sell opportunities.

discovery tool—A tool used by sales teams to guide value-based conversations by uncovering customer challenges and aligning solutions to those needs.

I

inside sales teams—Sales teams that nurture leads generated by marketing, assess purchase likelihood, and hand off top prospects to the main sales team.

internal rate of return (IRR)—The discount rate at which an investment's net present value equals zero, used to evaluate the profitability of investments.

M

marketing automation platforms—Tools that automate top-of-funnel marketing activities like email campaigns and digital ads, generating leads and delivering value messaging.

N

net present value (NPV)—The difference between the present value of an investment's cash inflows and outflows, accounting for the time value of money.

O

operating expenses (OpEx) savings—Reductions in day-to-day operational costs such as salaries, utilities, and maintenance.

outside-in business case—A business case created using publicly available information, typically early in the sales cycle when internal data isn't available.

P

payback period—The time it takes to recover the initial investment in a project through cash flows.

product marketing teams—Teams responsible for go-to-market strategies, including product positioning, pricing, and supporting sales and customer success teams.

productivity improvement—Strategies to increase output or efficiency while maintaining or reducing resource input, enhancing competitiveness and profitability.

R

retrieval augmented generation (RAG)—An AI system combining information retrieval with generative AI models to provide more accurate and relevant responses.

return on investment (ROI)—A financial measure comparing the profit generated by an investment to its cost, typically expressed as a percentage.

S

sales account team—Teams managing customer relationships, including account executives, solution architects, and customer success managers.

sales funnel—A framework that visualizes a buyer's journey, from awareness to purchase and renewal, helping track customer engagement and retention.

T

throughput—The rate at which a process or system produces output within a given time frame, often used as a measure of efficiency.

total cost of ownership (TCO)—The total cost of owning and maintaining an asset, including purchase, maintenance, and operational costs over its life cycle.

U

unit testing—Software testing focused on validating isolated units of source code to ensure expected behavior.

V

value automation tools—Software that automates parts of the business case process, such as ROI calculations and value narrative creation.

value baseline report—A reassessment of a business case based on the final scope and timing of a technology investment, aligning expected business outcomes with real conditions.

value benchmark—A quantitative measure tied to a value driver, used to demonstrate the impact of a solution based on industry standards or past customer outcomes.

value category—A set of value drivers that align with a specific business objective, such as recruiting in an HR solution.

value consultants/value engineers—Experts who build ROI models, conduct business cases for strategic deals, and engage with customer leadership.

value discovery—The process of identifying all factors needed to estimate the business value of a technology investment, including customer goals, challenges, and desired outcomes.

value driver—A quantifiable business outcome that highlights the value of a solution, usually including a description, formula, and industry benchmark.

value enablement services—Services supporting customers' adoption of value concepts, focusing on awareness, change management, and education.

value intelligence—Insights and correlations between value metrics, product usage, and sales data throughout the customer life cycle.

value management (VM)—Coordinating customer-facing functions to help customers realize the business value of solutions, driving revenue outcomes like deal wins and renewals.

value management programs—Organized activities designed to ensure value realization and improve revenue outcomes through a structured approach.

value messaging—Communications that emphasize the business impact of a solution, aligning it with customer objectives rather than focusing on product features.

value model—A mathematical model that calculates value metrics like ROI, productivity, and cost savings by combining investment costs and benefits.

value realization assessment—Post-deployment evaluations of the business impact of a solution, validating the expected value or defending the investment for contract renewals.

value selling programs—Strategic efforts to train and equip sales teams to communicate the business value of solutions, including sales process definitions, training, and incentives.

value tree—A structured framework that breaks down value categories like revenue growth or cost reduction into specific value drivers, illustrating business impact.

Acknowledgments

For more than two decades, we have been privileged to work with a group of pioneers who have helped define the theory and practice of value management. It is amazing that this small community of value management leaders has created such a powerful global network, and we are delighted to have built strong professional and personal relationships with many in this cohort. It is their hard work and leadership in delivering valuable business outcomes for enterprises across a range of industries that forms the foundation of the principles we have presented in this book.

Our team is especially grateful for the value management leaders who provided their personal insights, guidance, and inspiration for this book. Heartfelt thanks to Rob Thomas, senior vice president of software solutions and chief commercial officer at IBM; Patty Morrison, former CIO of Motorola and Cardinal Health and currently serving on the board of directors for Splunk, Baxter, and several other companies; Nick Mehta, CEO of Gainsight; Yousuf Khan, Partner, Ridge Ventures, and formerly CIO of Pure Storage; Madhav Thattai, COO, Salesforce AI; Ginna Raahauge, chief commercial officer at WWT; Bob Lim, executive vice president and CIO at San Jose State University; Paul Randlesome, GVP of value management at Silver Peak (now Aruba-HPE); and Sam Bouhdary, programs specialist, ServiceNow. A special shoutout also to Rob Bracken, our trusted technical writer and editor, who helped smooth the edges off our rough drafts and helped organize and clarify our disparate ideas, concepts, and theories.

Each of these contributors were kind enough to set aside time in their busy schedules to discuss the concepts presented in this book and share their personal and professional experiences and perspectives. Lastly, kudos to our friends and colleagues at Mainstay, who have partnered with many value management pioneers over the past 20 years, contributing their genuine passion for our industry and helping build a thriving community of value management leaders.

We also would like to thank the Wiley publishing team, including Kenyon Brown, John Sleeva, and Moses Ashirvad and their full editorial team, whose experienced eye helped position our manuscript to the business audience, improved our final editing of the manuscript, and provided valuable commercial and publication expertise.

Finally, we would like to thank our families and friends for putting up with the lost weekends over the months we spent writing, collaborating, and debating the content in this book. We promise to make up for the lost time once the book is published!

About the Authors

Craig LeGrande is the founder and CEO of Mainstay, a company that helps technology innovators quantify and communicate the business value of their solutions. Craig coauthored (along with Jeb Dasteel, Chief Customer Officer of Oracle, and author and professor Amir Hartman) the best-selling book *Competing for Customers* (Pearson FT Press, 2016). Craig also coauthored (along with Hartman) *Ruthless Execution II* (Pearson FT Press, 2015), which explores how agile businesses thrive in the digital economy.

Prior to Mainstay, Craig worked at Cisco Systems, leading its sales consulting practice for the automotive industry, and spent nearly a decade at Accenture in management consulting and software development roles. Craig earned an MBA from the Tuck School of Management at Dartmouth College and a Bachelor of Science with Honors in electrical engineering from the University of Florida.

Venky Lakshminarayanan, known to many colleagues and friends as LV, is president and chief revenue officer at Cron AI, a pioneer in AI-based 3D perception technology. With over two decades of experience at companies ranging from startups to global technology leaders, Venky brings deep expertise in business transformation, go-to-market strategies, customer success, and value management. Before joining Cron AI, he served as global head of Strategy and Strategic Value Advisory at ServiceNow. In that role, he was responsible for scaling the company's value management program, helping grow sales ten-fold from millions to billions of dollars. Venky also held key leadership positions at Tech Mahindra and Mainstay. He attended the University of California, Berkeley Haas School of Business, earned an MBA from SP Jain Institute of Management and Research in India, and a Bachelor of Engineering degree from BITS, Pilani, India.

Index